CONTENTS

P9-CQS-540

Acknowledgements

The author takes his hat off to the following for giving willingly their knowledge, time and experience to make this book a reality.

Friends and colleagues: Herbert Altman, DeWitt Bodeen, Eddie Brandt, Ben Carbonetto, Carol Carey, Lewis Chambers, John Cocchi, Jay Coppolo, Mary Corliss, David Croom, Critt Davis, Leonard de Cicco, A. Wymer "Skip" Gard, Mike Hawks, Richard Hudson, Lloyd Ibert, William Kenly, Al Kilgore, Don Koll, Dick Ledwith, Albert Lord, Leland Lowther, Don McConnell, Ed McDonald, Leonard Maltin, Francis Masone, Gunnard Nelson, Arthur Nicholson, Wayne Nordeen, John W. M. Phillips, Robert Pinotti, Adam Reilly, Marc Ricci, Vito Russo, Markku Salmi, Elmer Showers, Alexander Soma, Romano Tozzi, Gerald Turnbull, Jim Watters, Douglas Whitney, Malcolm Willits, Bill Wolfe *and* Dion McGregor whose still collection was the inspiration for this book. I would also like to thank my agents Dieter L. Klein and Jane Gregory.

Institutions and shops: Cinemabilia (NYC); Collector's Bookstore (Hollywood); British Film Institute/Still Dept. (London); Eddie Brandt's Saturday Matinée (North Hollywood); Hollywood Revue (Hollywood); Memory Shop (NYC); Museum of Modern Art/Film Stills Archive (NYC); Jerry Orlanger's Stills (NYC).

Studios and networks: American Broadcasting Company (ABC); Anglo-Amalgamated Film Distributors; British Broadcasting Corp. (BBC); British International; British Lion; British National; Cinerama Releasing Corp.; Columbia Broadcasting Company (CBS); Columbia Pictures; Commonwealth United Corp.; Compton-Tetcli; Continental Distributing, Inc.; Dixie National; Ealing Productions; First National; Gainsborough; Gaumont British; Grand Productions; Grove Press-Evergreen Films; Janus Films, Inc.; London Films; Lopert Pictures Corp.; Metro-Goldwyn-Mayer; Monogram; National Broadcasting Company (NBC); New Line Cinema; New World Films; Paramount Pictures; the Rank Organization; Republic Pictures; RKO-General Corp.; Hal Roach Productions; Steinmann-Baxter Productions; Twentieth Century-Fox; Two Cities; UFA; United Artists Corp.; Universal Pictures; Andy Warhol Productions; Warner Bros. Pictures; Warner Bros. Cartoons, Inc.

Introduction

Impersonation, n. Act or instance of impersonating, or state of being impersonated; personification; investment with personality; representation in a personal form, or an instance of it; dramatic representation.

Impersonation of the opposite sex has always been a fascinating subject. The practice has come down through the ages in many forms, and is significant to any study of mythology, religion, anthropology, psychology or social behaviour. As this brief introduction will show, drag did not begin with the movies but has been with us since ancient times, as part of individual behaviour—or as entertainment.

The "drag" pictures in this book cover seven decades and, in their own way, represent not only the actor's art of disguise but also offer us a microcosm of film history—one of the twentieth century's most exciting art forms, which has also left us a permanent record of the changing face of culture and society. Movies reflect our perceptions and customs from an age of public innocence to the new morality of the 1980s. Role-switching, disguises, masquerades and sexual transition are shown here in every form imaginable. This introduction does not pretend to be a comprehensive history of drag, merely providing a little information for the pictures that follow.

History abounds in examples of impersonation. Here are a few to ponder over:

The beautiful boy-priest Varius Avitus, renamed Elagabalus after his god (also known as Heliogabalus), became emperor of the Roman Empire at the age of fourteen. He was probably the greatest female impersonator of his time. Dressed as a girl, he would give dazzling dance displays before the populace but, if you were not totally enthralled by his performance, you ran the risk of being put to death. He was more vicious than any of his predecessors and his perverted antics were to bring about his downfall. In the year AD 222 he was assassinated, at the age of eighteen.

Julius Caesar, Nero, and Commodus—among other Roman emperors—enjoyed dressing as women and wore make-up, perfume, jewels and fine silks. These men sometimes impersonated heroines of mythology in public spectacles, and often continued the practice in their private lives.

In many primitive societies around the globe priests and witch-doctors often resorted, and still do, to female garb for certain pagan rites.

"Mumming" was an old English custom in which a man and his wife would swop roles when visiting their friends during the Christmas season. This tradition was adopted in America and, even today, mumming is still observed in some parts of New England.

Everyone learns in school that, in Shakespeare's time, boys played the female roles on stage, but the reason is often overlooked. Previously, the powerful Roman Catholic Church had pronounced that it was immoral for women to appear on stage. Because of the restrictions placed on them during this period, dramatists adjusted their plots and the relationships of their characters to comply with this censorship. Impersonation was thus one of the mainstays of Elizabethan and Jacobean theatre. These boy-actors became extremely proficient at assuming the mannerisms, vocal qualities, body gestures and movements of women. The word "drag", as used in the context of sexual impersonation, is thought to have its origins at this time. It probably started as a colloquialism with which audiences used to hail the entrance of the boy-actor as he came on stage, his gown dragging behind him. By the eighteenth century the arts had escaped the clutches of the Church and women began to appear on the stage. For a number of years, during this transitional period, there was bitter rivalry between the women and the boys whom they were replacing.

In Japan women had performed on the stage for only a short time before the authorities banned this practice in the name of public morality. These women were also succeeded by boys who simulated feminine mannerisms. Today, Kabuki theatre still upholds this tradition. Eventually women returned to the theatre forming all-female troupes of singers and dancers. And, like the Kabuki, these ladies would play opposite sex roles with great artistry.

Outside the theatre, interesting examples of impersonation cropped up in various parts of the world. The mother of the Frenchman François Timoléon Choisy often entertained Louis XIV. She constantly dressed her son as a girl during his youth and made him appear at court in this manner. His exuberant escapades finally resulted in his expulsion. Years later he became a religious convert and travelled to the Far and Middle East. He wrote many historical and religious works which are, however, overshadowed by his notorious memoirs of his early court life.

During the reign of Louis XV another young man became a court favourite as a lady. The Chevalier d'Eon, who also did some spying for the king, à la Mata Hari, kept up the masquerade all his life. Only on his death did the secret become public. The word "eonism" (the tendency to adopt the mental attitude and habits and costume of the other sex) derives from his name.

Even though women were becoming accepted as permanent figures in the theatre, composers such as Handel still wrote music for young boys with fine soprano voices. His operas are full of marvellous parts (and arias) for them. Who would have guessed that a new tradition would evolve from this? Women began singing these originally male roles and they are now exclusively sung by female sopranos. Known as "trouser roles" they can be found for example in the works of Mozart (*The Marriage of Figaro, Cosi fan Tutte*); Gluck (*Orpheus*); Beethoven (*Fidelio*); Rossini (*Semiramide*); Verdi (*Un Ballo in Maschera, La Forza del Destino, Rigoletto*); Moussorgsky (*Boris Gudounov*); Johann Strauss (*Die Fledermaus*); Wagner (*Tannhäuser*); Donizetti (*Lucrezia Borgia*); Offenbach (*The Tales of Hoffman*); Meyerbeer (*Les Huguenots*); and Gounod (*Faust*).

During the American revolutionary war one Deborah Sampson Gannett joined the Continental forces under the name of "Robert Shurtleff" and fought for almost two years with the Fourth Massachusetts Regiment. When she was wounded in battle the truth was discovered and she was immediately discharged from service.

During the late nineteenth century a laundress in Custer's Seventh Cavalry, known as "Mrs Nash", married several times but never accompanied her husbands when they were transferred to other posts. It was quite a shock to learn, when she died, that she was not, in fact, a woman!

Meanwhile, in the theatres of France, Italy, Germany, England and America, women were receiving tremendous acclaim for their performances in works by the leading dramatists of their day. Women were finally being recognised as fine performers and were exacting their revenge for all the years of neglect—by playing parts written for boys. Sarah Bernhardt's slimness was a definite aid to her portrayals of boys in over twenty plays, the most famous of which was Rostand's *L'Aiglon* in which she played Napoleon's doomed heir. Later this became a vehicle for Maude Adams in America, who was also to introduce *Peter Pan* to US audiences. Other notables of the day who played men with verve and polish were Vesta Tilley, Della Fox, Kathleen Clifford and Billie Burke.

Male drag had by no means disappeared, however. Brandon Thomas' farce *Charley's Aunt* opened in London in 1892, with William Penley in the title role. The next year Etienne Girardot played it in New York, and successfully revived it in 1906. It has had continual revivals in both countries ever since, with actors like José Ferrer, John Mills and Vincent Price, among many others, in the title role. This perennial comedy has survived both plot and period alterations, and even the addition of songs when Frank Loesser made it *Where's Charley?* in 1948. Because it is an "old chestnut" of the theatre, its five filmed versions and two television productions receive special attention in this book.

The popular travelling all-male minstrel shows included men like Lew Dockstader who successfully played women in comedy sketches. Drag became a prominent aspect of vaudeville and music hall entertainment. James Cagney, famed for his tough gangster characterisations in films, began his career as a "chorus girl" in vaudeville.

Julian Eltinge, the greatest female impersonator of his day, started off in the minstrel shows produced by George M. Cohan. He was a great favourite with women and would gently mock them with carefully executed "asides" which delighted his audiences. After a decade of theatrical successes Eltinge entered the movies in 1917.

Attitudes have changed over the years and so have the interpretations. The theatrical practice of women playing boys made an easy transfer to the silent screen, but actresses in such roles often maintained their femininity. The audiences of that time wanted it that way. A good example is Elizabeth Bergner's portrayal of Rosalind in the film version of Shakespeare's *As You Like It*. The audience never forgot that she was a woman masquerading as a boy to fool her lover. The fact that her lover couldn't see through her disguise didn't matter. It is interesting to compare Bergner with, for example, Judy Holliday or Anne Heywood (who played drag parts much more realistically), or, alternatively, with professional male entertainers who approach drag in a "camp" way, such as Britain's Danny La Rue. He is one of the biggest stars in the British Isles and has brought drag entertainment back to the family audiences that used to frequent the vaudeville halls. He has performed many shows over the years as well as appearing in television specials. When La Rue acted in *Charley's Aunt* on the BBC, he played the part of the aunt as a truly glamorous figure.

As I have already mentioned, this brief outline of drag can only serve as an introduction to the illustrations and gives just a hint of the vast variety to be found in the fascinating field of role-switching and impersonation. The pictures on the following pages, collected from the world of entertainment, show what drag is really all about—indeed, the pictures say it all . . .

CHARLEY'S AUNT—
The Old Chestnut

CHARLEY'S AUNT

Brandon Thomas' polished farce *Charley's Aunt* is surely "the old chestnut" of the theatre. It has been filmed five times (four American; one British) and has received two television productions (one American; one British).

The plot concerns a young nobleman, Lord Fancourt Babberly, at Oxford, who comes to the aid of his fellow students (Charley and Jack) by disguising himself as Charley's wealthy aunt from Brazil, Donna Lucia d'Alvardorez, to act as a chaperon for the two girls to whom they wish to propose marriage. Not only does Babberly enjoy embracing these young ladies at every chance he gets (to the annoyance of the boys) but also finds himself being pursued by a university don and the father of one of the girls.

SYD CHAPLIN became film's first Charley's Aunt in 1925 (opposite) while CHARLIE RUGGLES, here being kissed by June Collyer, did the first talkie in 1930. England's ARTHUR ASKEY performed in a version in modern dress called *Charley's "Big Hearted" Aunt* (1940) and JACK BENNY pinched Edmund Gwenn's cheek in his 1941 re-make.

RAY BOLGER starred in Frank Loesser's musical-comedy *Where's Charley?* on Broadway in 1948 (Norman Wisdom played the part in London) and also in the filmed version of 1952 (shown here with Robert Shackleton).

ART CARNEY was well received in the title role in CBS's Playhouse 90 production on American television in 1957(left). And when female impersonator DANNY LA RUE did his colour TV version for BBC's Play of the Month in 1969, he abandoned corkscrew curls and crinolines for a look that was decidedly *not* that of a "maiden aunt"(p.1).

SOME
LIKE IT HOT–
The Classic Drag Film

SOME LIKE IT HOT

Other than the various versions of *Charley's Aunt*, no film expanded on a single joke — utilising drag throughout the entire movie — more than Billy Wilder's delightful lampoon *Some Like It Hot* (1959). This fabulous farce is indeed the classic drag film of all time.

The prolonged masquerade was kept constantly alive by brilliant direction of the nimble script and outstanding acting from the principals.

After witnessing the St Valentine's Day massacre two musicians flee Chicago as members of an all-girl band heading by train for a club date in Miami. TONY CURTIS (left) was saxophonist Josephine, while JACK LEMMON (right) became Daphne, a bass violinist. Their misadventures with the girls are further complicated when they fall for sassy Sugar Kane (Marilyn Monroe), the band's vocalist.

Curtis romances Monroe à la Cary Grant while being the girl's confidant when masquerading as Josephine. Lemmon, meanwhile, is pursued by millionaire Joe E. Brown (himself a fine drag artist in his heyday). Their gay fandango is a highlight. In the final scene Lemmon confesses that he can't marry Brown because he's really a *man*! Replies Brown: "Well... nobody's perfect!"

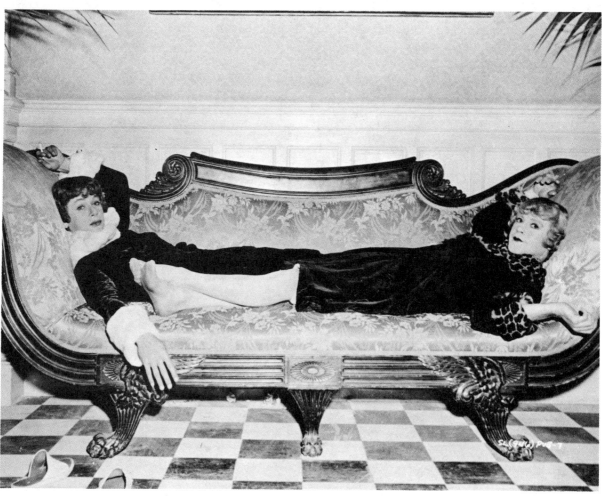

THE
COMEDIANS

VESTA TILLEY

The great turn-of-the-century drag artiste, **VESTA TILLEY**, was not only a music hall headliner but made several British films between 1900 and 1916. This is a typical portrait of the period.

WALLACE BEERY

WALLACE BEERY was equally comfortable as a comedian or dramatic actor. Between 1914 and 1916 Beery appeared in about thirty short comedies as a Swedish maid called "Sweedie". Here the portrait shows the whimsical side of this actor's unique characterisation. The scene, from *Dreamy Sweedie* (1914), illustrates the kind of situation Sweedie got "herself" into — caught by her employer smoking a cigar instead of sweeping up.

FATTY ARBUCKLE

ROSCOE "FATTY" ARBUCKLE was one of America's greatest slapstick comedians. For sheer variety — and side-splitting humour — Fatty often dressed as a girl.

Here he can be seen in an early short — a vision in a flowered-print and chequered coat. In the two-reeler *That Minstrel Man* (1915) Fatty made a robust black woman!

CHARLIE CHAPLIN

CHARLIE CHAPLIN — the greatest of silent comedians — in *A Woman* (1915) makes enemies of Charles Insley and Billy Armstrong who would like to kill him. He seeks refuge in an upstairs bedroom where he discovers women's clothes. Edna Purviance, daughter of one of the men, is astounded at Charlie's "change" but helps him find a razor. Later, he charms his two pursuers who are none the wiser.

MARY PICKFORD

MARY PICKFORD, one of the biggest comedians of the silent era, masqueraded as a boy in many films to the delight of her fans.

In *Poor Little Peppina* (1915) Mary dons boy's clothing for her own safety in a rough section of New York City while trying to locate her parents.

The Hoodlum (1919) presented Mary as a Park Avenue snob who disguises herself as a boy to learn about slum life.

JULIAN ELTINGE

JULIAN ELTINGE, the great female impersonator of vaudeville and the theatre, was finally lured to films in 1917 by Adolph Zukor. He was a popular success as the trade advertisement indicates. The plots of his films always contained some pretext by which he could make the transformation into female attire plausible.

His first starring role was in the delightful comedy *The Countess Charming* (1917) with Florence Vidor as the *ingénue*. This was followed by *The Widow's Might* (1917) whose cast also included Vidor (in white hat) and Gustav von Seyffertitz (in cap).

In 1918 he donated his time to a propaganda picture, entitled *War Relief*, made to stimulate the second Liberty Bond drive. The cast included Theodore Roberts, William S. Hart, Douglas Fairbanks and Mary Pickford.

In one of his last starring vehicles, *Madame Behave* (1925), Eltinge, disguised as a mystery woman, consoles Ann Pennington in this scene which took place before the double wedding fadeout.

Julian Eltinge

One of the last highly successful stage stars
to enter motion pictures. His three pictures by the
Lasky - Paramount have been such a sensat-
ional success that he is now classed with
Fairbanks   as a draw-
and Pickford   ing card.

Needless to
say he will

remain in
pictures

BEN TURPIN

BEN TURPIN, the earliest of the great slapstick comedians, began his screen antics in 1907. His many one- and two-reelers in the teens included several of Wallace Beery's ''Sweedie'' comedies. Turpin's strabismic gaze made his one of the most famous faces in the movies. Here he can be seen as a sheriff in disguise in *Sheriff Nell's Tussle* (1918), with Polly Moran in the title role.

One of Turpin's biggest hits was *The Shriek of Araby* (1923), a five-reeler, satirising the image Rudolph Valentino was then projecting on the screen. The scene portrait shows him as an alluring houri.

BOBBY VERNON

BOBBY VERNON, one of the original Keystone Kops, appeared in loads of one- and two-reelers during the teens and twenties. He got into drag often but was never funnier than in his spoof of Theda Bara's successful 1917 version of *Cleopatra*.

GLORIA SWANSON

Impersonations were part of GLORIA SWANSON's stock in trade in the early comedies she made for Mack Sennett. When she became a star under the aegis of Cecil B. de Mille she delighted co-workers with her mimicry of the director's famous stance (shown here in 1919).

In Allan Dwan's *Manhandled* (1924), Swanson did impersonations of Bea Lillie and Charlie Chaplin in the drawing-room scene. On the set Dwan borrowed the Chaplin moustache from Gloria!

By the time she starred in *The Humming Bird* (1924) Swanson was a past master. As Toinette, a fearless Apache pickpocket — dubbed "the humming bird" by the denizens of the Montmartre underworld because of her agility — she slips easily by the police, who are looking for a young man.

When she returned to the screen in *Sunset Boulevard* (1950), Swanson repeated her brilliant Chaplin imitation for a new generation of fans.

HARRY LANGDON

Veteran vaudevillean **HARRY LANGDON** was
a natural for silent pictures. He developed a
unique screen image that endeared him to his
fans. He was also a brilliant satirist as
evidenced here in his burlesque of the great
sea adventures, which he labelled *The Sea
Squawk* (1924).

LAUREL & HARDY

STAN LAUREL and OLIVER HARDY both injected humorous "drag" bits into their comedies before they teamed up together and many times during their brilliant association.

As seen here in *Get 'em Young* (1926) Stan does a fantastic drag impersonation. In *Twice Two* (1933) "the boys" played themselves and their wives! The results were hilarious.

Near the end of their association they were carnival musicians who con some con men with snappy card playing in *Jitterbugs* (1943) (opposite top).

In a different vein "the boys" were lovingly impersonated by SUSANNAH YORK (as Laurel) and BERYL REID (as Hardy) as two lesbians in drag for a costume party in the staggering comedy-drama *The Killing of Sister George* (1968).

BEA LILLIE

BEA LILLIE did expert impersonation work in *Exit Smiling* (1926) as a wardrobe mistress for a touring repertory company who gets ex-bank teller Jack Pickford hired as a stagehand. On the side, she coaches him for the villain's part which he eventually gets. However, when the show plays his hometown Bea dons male attire and goes on as the melodrama's villain opposite Doris Lloyd's heroine.

Are You There? (1930) found Bea as a lady detective with a penchant for unusual disguises (like that of a Chinese) when hired by a duke's son to prevent the marriage of his father to a gold-digging phoney countess.

SYD CHAPLIN

SYD CHAPLIN, after becoming film's first Charley's Aunt, again used female impersonation to advantage in these two comedies.

In *The Man on the Box* (1925) wealthy bachelor Syd learns that a butler serving a formal party at his sweetheart's home is actually an enemy agent after some of her father's plans. Syd, disguised as a lady's-maid, may fool Theodore Lorch but not the knowing housekeeper.

The farce *Oh, What a Nurse!* (1926) had Syd as a cub reporter substituting for an advice-to-the-lovelorn columnist who advises a girl not to marry the man her uncle is forcing upon her. Later, as the plot — and slapstick — thicken, dressed in nurse's garb he gets involved with rumrunners and eventually marries the girl himself.

CHARLEY CHASE

CHARLEY CHASE had one of the great comic faces in the movies. His henpecked expression held him in good stead in some 200 shorts. He is seen here vamping the young Oliver Hardy in *Be Your Age* (1926), directed by Leo McCarey.

REGINALD DENNY

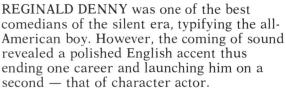

REGINALD DENNY was one of the best comedians of the silent era, typifying the all-American boy. However, the coming of sound revealed a polished English accent thus ending one career and launching him on a second — that of character actor.

1926 saw him in drag twice. On the eve of his wedding, in *What Happened to Jones*, Denny joins a poker party that is raided and escapes to a Turkish bath on ladies' night, returning home in female garb, befuddling maid ZaSu Pitts.

According to his uncle's will in *Take it From Me*, bankrupt Denny will inherit a department store if he can run it profitably for three months. During this trial period he is forced to disguise himself as a model in the store's fashion show to evade the process server.

MABEL NORMAND

MABEL NORMAND, undisputed queen of slapstick comedy, is seen here in a scene from a 1926 two-reeler disguised as a World War I soldier. Also, visiting the set are Our Gang members Mickey Daniels, Johnny Downs, Allen "Farina" Hoskins, Scooter Lowry, Jackie Condon and Joe Cobb.

CHESTER CONKLIN

When Paramount was searching for a bright, young newcomer to play the coveted role of Lorelei Lee in Anita Loos' *Gentlemen Prefer Blondes* (1928), former Keystone Kopper **CHESTER CONKLIN** — complete with walrus moustache — auditioned for the part to the delight of the Press. Luckily, he didn't get it. Conklin, it seems, had already been cast as a judge in the picture but his publicity stunt was worth its weight in gold to the studio.

MARION DAVIES

MARION DAVIES, one of the brightest comediennes of the screen, was an accomplished mimic. This talent was incorporated into many of her screenplays.

In *The Cardboard Lover* (1928) Marion is hired by a French tennis champion to keep him and his unfaithful girl friend (Jetta Goudal) apart. The American girl does her job so well — which included posing as a bellboy and, at one point, the French girl herself — that the Frenchman marries her instead.

Marianne (1929), in both its silent (bottom left) and talkie (top right) versions, had Marion play a French innkeeper who tries to keep a pet pig from being slaughtered. American Army private Lawrence Gray (in the talkie version) tries to help her but is later imprisoned. She returns the favour — masquerading as a French lieutenant — by interceding on his behalf.

Trick photography made Marion a Lilliputian figure with a chorus of men dressed as Grenadier Guards in the delightful number "Tommy Atkins on Parade" from *Hollywood Revue of 1929*.

ARTHUR LAKE

ARTHUR LAKE got a lot of mileage out of using female impersonation in his silent and talkie films. In the movie version of Carl Ed's comic strip *Harold Teen* (1928), Lake as Harold disguises himself as a girl to flirt with Mary Brian during "no date week" on campus when boys were not allowed such privileges. But he had trouble keeping his skirt on.

Lake also won fame as comic strip character Dagwood Bumstead in Chic Young's Blondie series. In *Blondie Goes Latin* (1941) Lake dons female attire on a Latin American cruise to keep an eye on Penny Singleton (Blondie) as she dances with Tito Guizar. *Blondie Hits the Jackpot* (1949) gave him another opportunity but Lloyd Corrigan and Jerome Cowan are not fooled for long.

BUSTER KEATON

The great **BUSTER KEATON** seldom ventured into female garb in his silent comedies but when he reached talkies he thought doing so would liven up the proceedings.

In *Dough Boys* (1930) he was a man who joins the Army by mistake and eventually ends up in France where he and fellow soldier **PITZY KATZ** do a drag number for the camp show.

In *Sidewalks of New York* (1931) Keaton was a millionaire who tries to reform delinquents. Here is a scene from the "show" sequence with Keaton sitting on Cliff Edwards' lap.

EDDIE CANTOR

EDDIE CANTOR, a patsy for a fortune-telling gang in *Palmy Days* (1931), takes off with the booty and hides in the ladies' bathing facilities of a large bakery. With the gang in hot pursuit Eddie bakes the money in a loaf of bread, disguises himself as a girl to conceal his identity and fools everyone except the sceptical gymnastic instructor Charlotte Greenwood.

GORDON HARKER

GORDON HARKER, Britain's bright cockney comedian, enjoyed popularity similar to that of Fernandel in France and Toto in Italy, which means he was a regional favourite on stage and screen. In *Love on Wheels* (1932) Harker used female disguise to thwart thieves in a large department store. Leonora Corbett is not amused by Harker's chic pose.

HAROLD LLOYD

HAROLD LLOYD seldom used impersonation in his silent work. He may have felt it didn't fit the bashful American boy image he had created. He did, however, realise its comic value for others. In Lloyd's first two-reeler that introduced this horn-rimmed character, *Bumping into Broadway* (1919), GUS LEONARD (at right) for some unknown reason played a snooping female peering as the bouncer ejects delinquent tenant Bebe Daniels, and her suitor (Lloyd) from the boardinghouse.

Lloyd finally appeared in drag in his talkie *Movie Crazy* (1932) and seems to have been a bit clumsy. Here Constance Cummings is patching up his leg.

CICELY COURTNEIDGE

Droll British comedienne CICELY COURTNEIDGE scored one of her biggest hits in *Soldiers of the King* (1933), called *The Woman in Command* in the US. As a music hall star who wishes to wed Edward Everett Horton, a lieutenant in the King's guards, Cicely masquerades as a guard herself to gain acceptance from stern commanding officer Frank Cellier.

JIMMY DURANTE

A comedian as funny looking as **JIMMY DURANTE** has to be funnier when dressed up as a woman. Durante's vignette in the revue *The Hollywood Party* (1934) made comic hokum out of a tragic event — a woman going to her death in the French Revolution.

He was hysterically funny doing an Apache dance with Anthony Caruso in *You're in the Army Now* (1941).

THE MARX BROTHERS

A Night at the Opera (1935) provided the Marx Brothers with the one occasion when at least two of them together resorted to female impersonation. To help them reduce grand opera to low comedy **HARPO** and **CHICO MARX** become gypsy chorus girls for Verdi's *Il Trovatore* in what must be the zany trio's funniest film.

JOE E. BROWN

Comedian JOE E. BROWN provided riotously funny films to a generation of moviegoers. During his long career (1928-1963) he essayed female disguise with great flair, comic skill and professionalism. Brown played everything from a baby girl (see studio portrait), to the hilarious Flute in the play-within-a-play sequence of Shakespeare's *A Midsummer Night's Dream* (1935), seen here perched on James Cagney's knee.

He continued his drag activities in the 1940s when he went west in *Shut My Big Mouth* (1942), where he disguised himself as a woman to elude outlaws. Here he seems afraid he might enjoy hooking-up Adele Mara's dress. The same year he played an old woman in *The Daring Young Man*.

STUART ERWIN

During the mid-thirties Paramount asked some of its most popular players to pose as the character they most wanted to play on the screen. STUART ERWIN chose "Little Bo Peep" but decided to keep his own shoes and socks on for the still photographer.

THE RITZ BROTHERS

The **RITZ BROTHERS** made getting into drag an essential part of their antics in several of their mad comedies.

In *On the Avenue* (1937) **HARRY RITZ** does a parody of Alice Faye's Bowery Girl in the jazzy Irving Berlin production number ''Slumming on Park Avenue'', but the lady is not impressed.

The trio, dressed as scrubwomen, invade the YWCA in the backstage musical *You Can't Have Everything* (1937), and can be seen here with Alice Faye.

The following year Harry Ritz appeared as The Queen in a burlesque of Disney's *Snow White* in a bit of foolishness called *Kentucky Moonshine* (1938). Here the make-up men are putting on the final touches.

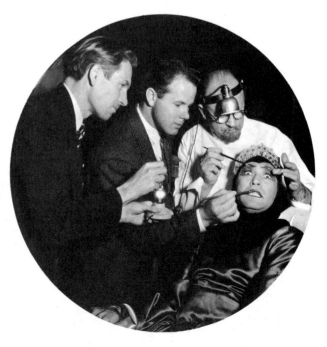

MICKEY ROONEY

In *The Adventures of Huckleberry Finn* (1937) MICKEY ROONEY delved into amateur theatricals as Shakespeare's heroine Juliet — seen here in the famous balcony scene.

THE THREE STOOGES

The THREE STOOGES (LARRY FINE, MOE HOWARD and JERRY "CURLY" HOWARD) always seemed out of place wherever they happened to be — or in whatever situation they happened to find themselves. That was their formula and make the most of it they did! Either separately or *en masse* these lunatic comics often got into drag.

In *Wee Wee Monsieur* (1938) the trio accidentally join the French Army and have to become harem girls to survive in the land of Tsimmis.

In *Rhythm and Weep* (1946) the boys and some girl entertainers are hired to do a show, but the Stooges end up doing the girls' number.

RED SKELTON

RED SKELTON, seen here with John Regan, seems to be enjoying his full-drag masquerade in the 1939 short *Seeing Red*.

Later, in *Bathing Beauty* (1944), Red, in order to be near the girl he loves, becomes one of Ann Codee's ballet pupils.

GRACIE FIELDS

GRACIE FIELDS, the warm, funny Lancashire lass who became England's biggest music hall star in the 1930s, also made many popular films. In *Shipyard Sally* (1939) Gracie played a saloon keeper who poses as an American singer to convince a lord to reopen the shipyard.

W. C. FIELDS

W. C. FIELDS as Cuthbert J. Twillie in *My Little Chickadee* (1940) prepares for his wedding night with his bride (Mae West) by bathing and primping in her boudoir. Little does he know that she has run off for an evening with the local masked bandit.

HUGH HERBERT

Character actor **HUGH HERBERT** — generally only part of a larger comic tapestry — played, in *La Conga Nights* (1940), not one but six roles. *Five* were female! In order to pay their rent, musicians and dancers in a boardinghouse open their own nightclub. Helping them along is a jazz-crazy tycoon, his four musical sisters and their nutty mother — all played by Herbert. Here he is as the mother.

WILL HAY

WILL HAY, a music hall star in England, was a comic who did not attain international status. Nevertheless, he was a big draw in Britain. In *The Black Sheep of Whitehall* (1941) Hay played a teacher who becomes involved with economics expert John Mills and, to save him from a nursing home run by spies, dons nurse's garb. Margaret Halstan is on the right.

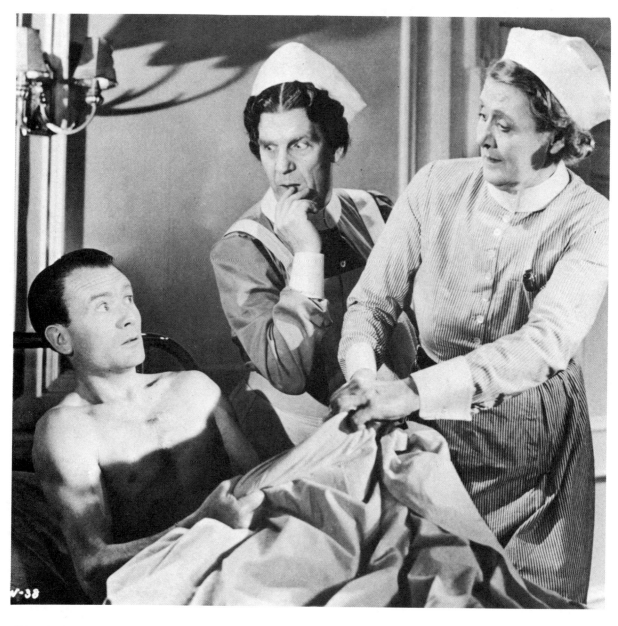

BOB HOPE

Comedian BOB HOPE has always known what audiences find funny and has, upon occasion, injected masquerade whether it be of the same or opposite sex. The Crosby-Hope-Lamour "Road" pictures were naturals for disguise as the portrait from *The Road to Morocco* (1942) (top left) indicates.

In *They Got Me Covered* (1943) Hope stops before the mirror to check himself as the daffy ex-newsman turned G-man in this spy comedy.

As entertainer Sylvester the Great he is captured, along with a princess, by buccaneers on the Spanish Main in *The Princess and the Pirate* (1944). When it is announced that all the men will walk the plank, Sylvester turns up as a gypsy wench but soon has to fight off a toothless pirate (Walter Brennan).

As the hapless racetrack tout in *The Lemon Drop Kid* (1951) Hope had one of his best roles. At one point he makes up as a sixty-year-old lady to escape detection from a mob big shot hot on his trail.

LOU COSTELLO

LOU COSTELLO often delved into the world of female impersonation for his madcap comedies. In *Lost in a Harem* (1944) Lou masqueraded as a harem cutie to fool villainous Douglass Dumbrille as Bud Abbott looks on.

In *Abbott and Costello Meet the Killer* (1949) Lou was a bellhop, suspected of murdering a guest, who masquerades as a chambermaid. Here he must play cards with house dick Abbott and two stiffs while warding off the amorous glances of Percy Helton.

JERRY LEWIS

One would think that female masquerade would be a natural ingredient in the comic foolishness of funnyman JERRY LEWIS, yet he seldom used it in his pictures.

A notable exception was his "drag" scene in his first starring movie, *At War with the Army* (1951). Dewey Robinson and Mike Kellin don't quite know what to make of this sassy "chick".

FERNANDEL

FERNANDEL, France's great domestic clown, agreed to become Bob Hope's co-star in *Paris Holiday* (1958). As two rival actors the wisecracking Hope and the miming Fernandel romped around a plotless picture in one sight gag after another. The French comic in drag, seen here with Hope, was one of them.

PETER SELLERS

PETER SELLERS in *The Mouse That Roared* (1959) played three roles; two male, one female. As Gloriana, the Grand Duchess of Grand Fenwick, Sellers issued the order to invade America, insisting, "I don't want anyone hurt."

As the world's richest and most eccentric man, Sellers in *The Magic Christian* (1969), donned many disguises in mad schemes to demonstrate that man can indeed be corrupted by money. He's seen here as a disco nun.

DANNY KAYE

DANNY KAYE, with his usual command of mimicry, outdid himself in *On the Double* (1961) as a meek US soldier who entertains his buddies with imitations of Hitler, Churchill and a host of others. He is so good that military intelligence nabs him for an important assignment — Operation Dead Pigeon. He is captured by the Nazis but before reaching Berlin escapes to a nightclub where he impersonates everyone from a Dietrich-type songstress (seen here) to a Luftwaffe pilot.

NORMAN WISDOM

British comedian **NORMAN WISDOM**'s frantic comedies have seldom done as well overseas. Here he is seen in *A Stitch in Time* (1963), one of his best, as a butcher's assistant masquerading as a nurse in order to visit a sick orphan.

PAUL LYNDE

PAUL LYNDE in *The Glass Bottom Boat* (1966) is one security guard (of an electronics plant) who takes his job seriously, especially where industrial spies are concerned. Lynde disguises himself as a woman to see what he can learn but locks horns with CIA agent Eric Fleming who was only being polite.

DANNY LA RUE

England's foremost female impersonator
DANNY LA RUE has popularised this art form
and made it respectable family entertainment.
His stage shows and television specials are a
tribute to his skill. La Rue's only film, the
wartime comedy *Our Miss Fred* (1971), was
never released in the US and did not do as
well as it should have in Britain. But at least
Danny La Rue made the movies! As an
entertainer drafted into the Army and sent to
France in 1940, La Rue makes his entrance in
a camp show just as the Germans take over
the town. Our "heroine" is saved from the
Gestapo by the overly attentive German
General Alfred Marks.

WOODY ALLEN

Crackpot intellectual WOODY ALLEN goes off to South America and ends up becoming a dictator of mythical San Marcos in his *Bananas* (1971). Cut from the final print of this gag-oriented comedy, unfortunately, was a drag scene in which Allen masqueraded as a bewitching señorita.

THE
COMEDIES

PEGGY

BILLIE BURKE made her motion picture debut, in Triangle's 1915 comedy *Peggy*, as a hoydenish American girl who visits her uncle in Scotland, spending much of the time in trousers.

PETER PAN

James M. Barrie's 1904 fantasy *Peter Pan* was subtitled "or, the Boy Who Wouldn't Grow Up", but the title character is always played by a woman, whether in straight, semi-musical or musical versions.

BETTY BRONSON was a charming Peter in the superb silent version of 1924, directed by Herbert Brenon. Here we see Peter worried that he will not find his shadow and, later, with Wendy (Mary Brian) in Never Never Land.

UNKNOWN SHORT

The value of the sight-gag, a mainstay of silent film comedies, was never more apparent than in this scene from an unknown short of the mid-teen period.

MONEY TALKS

OWEN MOORE chicly demonstrates in these two scenes from *Money Talks*, a 1926 farce, both the perils and benefits of impersonating the opposite sex. Disguised as a no-show female doctor he had hired for his resort hotel, Moore almost gets himself into a compromising situation with Ned Sparks. Later he pauses for a moment to enjoy the shapely Kathleen Key.

DER FÜRST VON PAPPENHEIM

In the 1927 German film *Der Fürst von Pappenheim* (*The Duke of Pappenheim*), CURT BOIS and MONA MARIS are vaudeville entertainers who perform a drag act. Later, Bois agrees to see a rich man (played by Hans Junkermann) after a performance and the fun begins.

After Bois, a Jew, fled his native Germany to work in the US, the Nazis used clips of his drag performance — to illustrate that Jews minced about in women's clothes — for propaganda purposes.

Bois is remembered today as the pickpocket in *Casablanca*.

FINDERS KEEPERS

Double drag appears in *Finders Keepers* (1928), a World War I comedy, when LAURA LA PLANTE as the colonel's daughter convinces Army private ARTHUR RANKIN to switch clothes with her, so she can see her boyfriend in the training camp before he is shipped overseas.

THREE WISE CLUCKS

Possibly the worst thing that can happen to someone in drag is to be exposed. This scene from a 1931 short subject entitled *Three Wise Clucks* is a perfect example. The players are unknown but the tension is very real.

GIRLS WILL BE BOYS

Continental star **DOLLY HAAS** appeared often in drag in her native Germany and did the same in England in 1934, when she appeared as a girl who posed as the grandson of a noble misogynist in *Girls Will Be Boys*. The young man on the receiving end is Esmond Knight.

SHE LOVES ME NOT

Razzle-dazzle cabaret dancer MIRIAM HOPKINS witnesses a murder and takes refuge in a Princeton dormitory in *She Loves Me Not* (1934). Collegiate Bing Crosby helps in her disguise as a male student, and she passes the ultimate test when Kitty Carlisle, the dean's daughter, drops in to see boyfriend Bing. Later, they are visited by gangster Warren Hymer who has been sent to "rub her out".

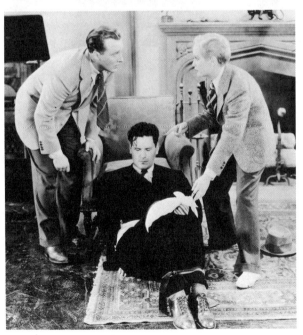

HIGH TIME

As a millionaire after a college degree in *High Time* (1960), **BING CROSBY** must make an appearance at a swanky party, dressed as a southern belle, to be accepted into the Xi Delta Pi fraternity. Here he is getting last-minute instructions from Richard Beymer.

BRINGING UP BABY

CARY GRANT, in Howard Hawks' 1938 farce *Bringing Up Baby*, was forced to wear Katharine Hepburn's négligé when the lady herself had his clothes sent to the laundry. Coming upon this vision May Robson could hardly believe her eyes!

I WAS A MALE WAR BRIDE

In Howard Hawks' *I Was a Male War Bride* (1949) French captain CARY GRANT marries American WAC lieutenant Ann Sheridan in Germany, the very day she is ordered to return home. He must masquerade as a WAC officer first to qualify as a "war bride" to gain entry into the US and, second, to be with his wife in the WAC billets in the meantime. The group scene shows seaman Kenneth Tobey checking the two war brides aboard.

OLD MOTHER RILEY

Between 1937 and 1952 British comedian ARTHUR LUCAN made about twenty comedies as washerwoman Mother Riley who gets herself into — and out of — all sorts of situations. In *Old Mother Riley MP* (1939) she is elected to the British Parliament by her tenement neighbours and is eventually made a minister. Here "she" addresses the House of Commons.

TURNABOUT

The joke in Thorne Smith's farcical *Turnabout* (1940) concerned **JOHN HUBBARD** and **CAROLE LANDIS** transferring to each other's bodies after muttering a few well-chosen words to a statue of Buddha. The misadventures that follow — like Hubbard showing Landis how to tie a cravat — were sometimes hilarious.

ALL-AMERICAN CO-ED

JOHNNY DOWNS, formerly a kid in the Our Gang comedies, masqueraded as a girl to meet lovely Frances Langford at a posh girl's school in *All-American Co-Ed* (1941).

LOVE CRAZY

Suave **WILLIAM POWELL** masqueraded as his own matronly sister in an attempt to foil divorce proceedings initiated by his wife, Myrna Loy, in *Love Crazy* (1941), sophisticated slapstick at its nimble best. Powell seems to have convinced Jack Carson and Gail Patrick but Myrna merely played along.

UP JUMPED THE DEVIL

MANTAN MORELAND is one character actor whom moviegoers probably do not remember by name but his face is unforgettable. His bulging eyes, shrill voice and comic delivery made him an asset to a host of ghost stories, mysteries and the Charlie Chan films.

But Moreland was a star in a little-known area of picture-making — the all-black films that were produced in the US for the nation's black audiences.

In the comedy *Up Jumped the Devil* (1941), produced by Dixie National, Moreland and his cohort Shelton Brooks are two out-of-work comedians trying to keep out of trouble. They pose as manservant and maid in order to get jobs on the estate of a wealthy woman.

SOUTH OF TAHITI, SONG OF THE ISLANDS & RAINBOW ISLAND

Drag in the form of comic relief sprang up in at least three South Seas musical comedies in the 1940s.

In *South of Tahiti* (1941) husky pearl hunters HENRY WILCOXON, ANDY DEVINE and BRODERICK CRAWFORD were made to contribute, under duress, to the native fête on a tiny Polynesian island or suffer the consequences. They performed!

Seaman JACK OAKIE doesn't like the idea of becoming reformed cannibal chief Billy Gilbert's bride-dinner in *Song of the Islands* (1942), and he seeks the protection of fellow sailor Victor Mature.

EDDIE BRACKEN was one of three sailors cast away on *Rainbow Island* (1944). When the native queen lies dying he covers for native girl Dorothy Lamour who's with one of the other sailors.

CLANCY STREET BOYS
&
HOLD THAT LINE

HUNTZ HALL, the irrepressible zany of the original Dead End Kids, followed the gang — along with Leo Gorcey — into the East Side Kids series. In *Clancy Street Boys* (1943) Huntz masqueraded as a girl in a chic boutique. From 1946 until 1957 the ever-changing gang became the Bowery Boys. In one of their films — *Hold That Line* (1952) — HUNTZ HALL, LEO GORCEY, BENNY BARTLETT, DAVID GORCEY and GILL STRATTON, JR got into campus drag. The handsome letterman is John Bromfield.

ABROAD WITH TWO YANKS

DENNIS O'KEEFE and WILLIAM BENDIX, two marines on furlough in Australia, masquerade as a couple of dowagers to elude MPs in the wartime farce *Abroad With Two Yanks* (1944). Both men are after the affections of Helen Walker, who only has eyes for John Loder. Later, O'Keefe creates pandemonium at a local charity bazaar when he pretends to see a mouse under the dress of Ethelreda Leopold.

At the camp Bendix becomes the star of the "Marine Follies" and his chorus "girls" include O'KEEFE, ARTHUR HUNNICUT (far left) and BILL MURPHY (far right).

GENIUS AT WORK

A part of the comedy *Genius at Work* (1945) satirised the popular radio programme "Queen for a Day". Master of ceremonies Ralph Edwards is confronted by **WALLY BROWN** and **ALAN CARNEY**, who seem a bit miffed by the powder treatment they have just received.

ADAM'S RIB

In *Adam's Rib* (1949), directed by George Cukor, Spencer Tracy and Katharine Hepburn were husband and wife lawyers on opposing sides of the same case. During the trial Hepburn accuses Tracy of male chauvinism in his tough treatment of her client JUDY HOLLIDAY (left) and the other woman in the case JEAN HAGEN (right).

To prove her point Kate asks the jury to look at each woman and imagine for a moment that they are men. Holliday can also be seen on the lot with Tracy.

KIND HEARTS
AND CORONETS

In *Kind Hearts and Coronets* (1949), the brilliant satire of Edwardian manners and morals, ALEC GUINNESS played all eight relatives whom kinsman Dennis Price sets out to murder so he can rightfully succeed to the family dukedom. One of the eight was Lady Agatha d'Ascoyne, an early suffragette.

THE COMEDIANS

Graham Greene's *The Comedians* (1967) was certainly not a comedy but rather a stark drama, focusing on a reign of terror in a Caribbean country under black dictatorship. ALEC GUINNESS, however, provided what little humour there was when he went undercover, at one stage, as a local laundress.

BELLES OF ST TRINIAN'S
&
BLUE MURDER AT ST TRINIAN'S

The hilarious British comedy *Belles of St Trinian's* (1954) gave **ALASTAIR SIM** the opportunity for a dual role. As Miss Millicent Fitton, the dowdy old-maid headmistress, he had to contend with the crazy antics of a bevy of horrible schoolgirls as well as her brother Clarence, a bookie, who planned to use the school and its facilities for his own purposes.

In one of its sequels, *Blue Murder at St Trinian's* (1957), Sim again was on hand as Miss Fitton, but was joined this time by **LIONEL JEFFRIES** as a jewel thief posing as a headmistress of a girls' polo team on a UNESCO tour of Europe. The loot is hidden in the ball!

CARRY ON CONSTABLE

KENNETH WILLIAMS (left) and CHARLES HAWTREY (right), two brilliant zanies of the hilarious British Carry On series, not only get a chance to join the force in *Carry On Constable* (1960) but soon find themselves working "undercover".

PEPE As one of the thirty-five film celebrities gathered to launch Mexican comedian Cantinflas as a Hollywood star in *Pepe* (1960), JACK LEMMON brought back to life his deliciously daffy Daphne of *Some Like It Hot* for this cameo scene in a parking lot.

THE SEVEN FACES OF DR LAO

Fantasy came to the old west in *The Seven Faces of Dr Lao* (1964) giving TONY RANDALL an opportunity to play eight roles. As the mysterious Chinese of the title, whose travelling circus entertains — and educates — inhabitants of a small town by performing revealing parables, Randall was delightful. When the script dipped into Greek mythology, he appeared (shown here) as the snake-haired Medusa. Make-up artist William Tuttle won an Oscar for his work in this film.

VIVA MARIA
&
JULES AND JIM

BRIGITTE BARDOT (left) and JEANNE MOREAU (right) were a pair of Marias in Louis Malle's revolutionary comedy *Viva Maria* (1965), set in a fictional Central American country.

Bardot is shown here disguised as a man to ride trains and plant explosives to further the cause.

Moreau masquerades as a boy in a capricious moment of Francois Truffaut's *Jules and Jim* (1962).

A FUNNY THING HAPPENED ON THE WAY TO THE FORUM

PHIL SILVERS and JACK GILFORD added their own particular brand of low-comedy style to the hijinks of *A Funny Thing Happened on the Way to the Forum* (1966). A frenzied look at Ancient Rome, it was full of gags, pratfalls, songs, disguises and mistaken identities. The pair can be seen here in drag, with Buster Keaton and Zero Mostel.

BEDAZZLED In *Bedazzled* (1967), a fantasy with a biting satirical edge, updating the Faust legend, timid café cook DUDLEY MOORE is offered seven wishes for his soul by the taller PETER COOK. The British comedy duo's buffoonery struck a serious note when they ridiculed the deportment of nuns.

FUZZ On a stake-out in a park hoping to snare a local rape artist, bungling Boston detectives **BURT REYNOLDS** and **JACK WESTON**, in *Fuzz* (1972), disguise themselves as a pair of unlikely nuns.

THOROUGHLY MODERN MILLIE

JAMES FOX in *Thoroughly Modern Millie* (1967) dons female attire to save Mary Tyler Moore, and other unfortunate girls, from a white-slave racket operating in a Chinatown brothel. But, as things happen, it's Moore, aided by Julie Andrews, who has to save Fox when the building catches fire.

THE RITZ

Tough guy JERRY STILLER in *The Ritz* (1976) is trying to carry out his dead father's wishes by killing his brother-in-law who is hiding out in a gay bath-house. After a climactic fight the unconscious Stiller is put into drag by the gay clientele and the cops are called to take him away.

HOUSE CALLS

WALTER MATTHAU in *House Calls* (1978) plays a sexually aggressive widowed doctor who discovers one morning, in a young woman's apartment, that his clothes have disappeared and he has to resort to her attire in order to get home.

THE DRAMAS

THE AMAZONS

MARGUERITE CLARK, one of the most popular stars of the teens, displayed considerable versatility in *The Amazons* (1917). Clark, centre, with ELSIE LAWSON, left, and HELEN GREENE, right, rebel against a male-dominated society when they decide to crash an all-male club.

DANGER, GO SLOW

Glamorous silent star **MAE MURRAY** resorted to male impersonation when she masqueraded as a young safe-cracker in *Danger, Go Slow* (1918).

HAMLET

Danish actress **ASTA NIELSEN** was not the first woman to portray Hamlet on the screen (Sarah Bernhardt had filmed the famous duel scene in 1900) but her 1920 Danish-German co-production was unique because it was based on the *Saxo Grammaticus* — the source Shakespeare had used — and not on the great bard's play. This "prince" of Denmark had been raised a man because of reasons of State and could not reveal her disguise — not even to Ophelia.

By all accounts it was an extraordinary work directed by her husband Svend Gade. Nielsen gave a striking performance as the doomed Dane.

FOOLISH WIVES

In his production of *Foolish Wives* (1922) ERICH VON STROHEIM played a lecherous adventurer posing as a Russian count in Monte Carlo. Preying on women of all stations (servants, half-wits, society ladies — all "foolish wives"), his repulsive characterisation reached its height in a strange drag ensemble — obviously accentuating decadence. With him is his accomplice Mae Busch.

DOWN TO THE SEA
IN SHIPS
&
LAWFUL CHEATERS

CLARA BOW, before becoming the vivacious "It" girl, began her career in films as the young Quaker girl who disguises herself as a boy to stow away on a whaling vessel in *Down to the Sea in Ships* (1923).

In 1925 Clara disguises herself as a boy in order to convince a gang of crooks to reform in *Lawful Cheaters*.

PONJOLA, MISS NOBODY & EASY PICKINGS

ANNA Q. NILSSON resorted to male impersonation in several of her silent films and in so doing paid careful attention to details of manner and dress.

In *Ponjola* (1923) she expertly disguised herself as a man to follow the man she loved, who was engaged to another woman, to South Africa.

Miss Nobody (1926) gave Nilsson another opportunity for male impersonation. To avoid the attentions of a roué she flees the city in drag, becoming involved with hoboes whose leader is Walter Pidgeon (actually an author gathering material for a book). Before she reverts to female attire, Nilsson has an amusing scene with small-town girl Louise Fazenda, who is smitten with the young lad.

The mystery-comedy *Easy Pickings* (1927) found Nilsson and companion Jerry Miley caught in the act while burglarising a mansion.

THE SILENT ACCUSER

ELEANOR BOARDMAN, in *The Silent Accuser* (1924), dons male attire to accompany her falsely convicted boy friend, who has just escaped from prison, to Mexico in search of the real murderer. Before the culprit is brought to justice, Eleanor — in a local cabaret dancing with vamp Edna Tichenor — learns that being in disguise has its disadvantages.

ALMOST A LADY

MARIE PREVOST played a fashion model in *Almost a Lady* (1926), a comedy-drama that included mistaken identity and impersonations of the same and opposite sex. Here Marie makes a dashing "gentleman" in formal male attire.

EVE'S LEAVES

In *Eve's Leaves* (1926) LEATRICE JOY was the tomboy daughter of a freighter captain stationed in a Chinese port. On shore she meets the son of a wealthy teaplanter (William Boyd) who, thinking she's a boy, teases her. Once the pair get involved with pirates aboard her father's vessel Eve gets sweet revenge by saving the young man's life more than once.

THE
CRYSTAL CUP
&
BRIGHT LIGHTS

When DOROTHY MACKAILL attends a social affair in *The Crystal Cup* (1927) (bottom left) everyone thinks she's a man, not only from her appearance, but from her manner as well. A confirmed man-hater, because of her father's cruel treatment of her mother, she is purposely devoid of all feminine mannerisms but by fade out, has found a man she can love.

The backstage story *Bright Lights* (1930) was in a lighter vein. Here Dorothy plays an actress who is leaving greasepaint and footlights to marry a wealthy man. Before going, however, she sings — in formal male attire — the song "I'm Just a Man About Town".

HIT OF THE SHOW

GERTRUDE OLMSTEAD, another twenties actress who resorted to male impersonation, illustrates what the well-dressed young man of 1928 was wearing in this scene portrait from Joe E. Brown's *Hit of the Show*.

BEGGARS OF LIFE

LOUISE BROOKS in *Beggars of Life* (1928) shoots her foster father in self-defence, disguises herself as a boy, and hides among a group of drifters in a hobo camp, their leader being played by Wallace Beery. He becomes her protector and when the police begin to close in he, aided by fellow tramps, helps make good her escape.

SULLIVAN'S TRAVELS

In Preston Sturges' sardonic look at himself, *Sullivan's Travels* (1941), **VERONICA LAKE** is a cynical, unemployed movie extra who joins discontented film director Joel McCrae on a trip through the hobo jungles of America searching for a meaningful movie project. For her own protection she spends much of the time disguised as a boy.

MOROCCO, BLONDE VENUS & SEVEN SINNERS

No one represented European chic in her Hollywood movies more than MARLENE DIETRICH. An expression of Josef von Sternberg's vision of the "eternal woman", Dietrich fascinated men and women alike, whether in beads, feathers, sequins or in black tux, as seen here in her first American film *Morocco* (1930).

In *Blonde Venus* (1932) the tux was white (with a touch of sequins) but by 1940 was exchanged for a naval uniform so she could sing "The Man's in the Navy" in *Seven Sinners*.

LITTLE WOMEN
&
SYLVIA SCARLETT

In George Cukor's beautiful adaptation of *Little Women* (1933) KATHARINE HEPBURN, as Jo, writes plays which are enacted in the parlour of their Concord, Massachusetts, home during the dark days of the Civil War. Joan Bennett played the heroine with Hepburn as the villain of the melodrama.

The switch from whimsy to serious male impersonation greeted Hepburn in Cukor's *Sylvia Scarlett* (1936). Her boy's haircut was the perfect touch. As a girl on the lam with her father, Hepburn masquerades as his son to avoid detection. All the problems that could arise when in a "drag" situation were presented: the *boy* hesitating before the Ladies' Room door; men she is interested in treating *him* like one of the boys. We also see a shot of her here on the set.

BLOOD MONEY

Blood Money (1933), a pre-Code melodrama filled with assorted underworld types, had a delicious air of decadence. Here George Bancroft, a racketeering bail bondsman, waiting for his mistress (a classy whorehouse madam), is confronted by SANDRA SHAW in male attire, complete with monocle, who needs a light for her cigar.

THE DEVIL DOLL

Escaped convict LIONEL BARRYMORE in *The Devil Doll* (1936) returns to Paris, disguised as an old lady, to track down those who sent him to Devil's Island. With "devil dolls" (humans and animals one-sixth their normal size) doing his bidding his enemies are unpleasantly eliminated. His other concern is that his daughter (Maureen O'Sullivan) marries well.

WINGS OF THE MORNING

In the prologue to *Wings of the Morning* (1937), Britain's first Technicolor feature, ANNABELLA is a gypsy girl who marries a lord but who is banished, upon his death, by occult means, for four generations.

She returns, reincarnated, disguised as a boy, to Lord Clontarf's estate, seeking sanctuary from the civil war in Spain. Here she stumbles upon Henry Fonda, the earl's Canadian nephew, who is training a thoroughbred called Wings of the Morning for the Derby at Epsom Downs. The rest is pure romance.

KING OF ALCATRAZ

In the excellent B-picture *King of Alcatraz* (1938), J. CARROL NAISH is a convict on the lam who resorts to female impersonation. So that he and his mob can make good their escape aboard a commandeered freighter, Naish's masquerade as an old lady is essential. He is shown on board with Virginia Dabney and infuriated captain Harry Carey.

ONE OF OUR AIRCRAFT IS MISSING

HUGH WILLIAMS, checking his disguise in the mirror, and Godfrey Tearle (in cap), are two members of a crashed bomber crew about to be smuggled out of Holland by members of the Dutch Resistance in the excellent British war melodrama *One of Our Aircraft is Missing* (1942).

A SONG TO REMEMBER

Chic **MERLE OBERON** was a beautiful Mme Dudevant (the notorious nineteenth century French novelist George Sand) who fancied shocking her contemporaries in male attire when not involved romantically with composer Frederic Chopin, in the quasi-biographical *A Song to Remember* (1945).

THE HOUSE ON 92ND STREET

It's not until the final moments of the excellent semi-documentary *The House on 92nd Street* (1945) that the FBI, and the audience, learn that SIGNE HASSO is actually "Mr Christopher", the notorious US Nazi agent the FBI had long been seeking. Here Hasso, attempting a getaway from the surrounded building, realises that the jig is up.

I VITELLONI

I Vitelloni (1953) was Federico Fellini's sardonic study of idle middle-class youth in post-war Italy. The mood of these bored unmarried young men without occupations, who live off parents, relatives and friends, can best be summed up from the expression on **ALBERTO SORDI**'s face when he attends, in drag, a local carnival masked ball.

THE MAGICIAN

INGRID THULIN, in Ingmar Bergman's opus *The Magician* (Swedish, 1959), plays Max von Sydow's wife, who spends much of her time disguised as his young male pupil. Here we see the travelling troupe of medicine-show performers seeking permission to play Stockholm. With Thulin and Sydow are Naima Wifstrand and Ake Fridell.

DR CRIPPEN
&
CUL-DE-SAC

After killing his domineering wife in *Dr Crippen* (1964), meek Donald Pleasence shaves off his moustache, and his mistress SAMANTHA EGGAR disguises herself as a boy, in an attempt to flee to America, but their plans are foiled by a suspicious ship's captain (James Robertson Justice).

In Roman Polanski's *Cul-de-sac* (1966) PLEASENCE was a weirdo who prefers transvestism to his nymphomaniacal young wife (Françoise Dorleac), before a group of wounded thugs terrorise their existence in a remote castle on England's northern coast.

SYLVIA

In *Sylvia* (1965) a private eye searching for background information on the fiancée of his wealthy client discovers that the young lady had been, among other things, a B-girl. PAUL GILBERT played Lola Diamond, the cigar-smoking madam of that bordello!

ULYSSES

MILO O'SHEA, as the uncertain Jew Leopold Bloom, gets some help with his hairdo from Maureen Toal during one of his weird fantasies in Joseph Strick's outstanding production of James Joyce's *Ulysses* (1967).

NO WAY TO TREAT A LADY

ROD STEIGER in *No Way to Treat a Lady* (1968) is a mother-haunted stage producer who employs many disguises (ranging from Irish priest to gay hairdresser) to meet, and ultimately kill, lonely women. Posing as a frightened barfly, Steiger sets a trap here for unsuspecting victim KIM AUGUST, who is actually a female impersonator (a fact not revealed in the plot). Perhaps director Jack Smight was testing his audience with this in-joke!

THE DAMNED

Luchino Visconti's spectacle of corruption and perversity *The Damned* (1969) focused on the first two years (1933-34) of Hitler's struggle to get the great German industrial families to support his quest for power. HELMUT BERGER, the heir to such a family empire, provides some entertainment at one stage with a superb drag impersonation of Marlene Dietrich.

Visconti delved into history for his depiction of the "night of the long knives". These orgy scenes accentuate the decadence that was becoming an embarrassment to Nazi Germany. Members of Ernst Röhm's homosexual SA (Storm Troopers) frolic in drunken gaiety before being massacred by the SS.

TRIPLE ECHO

Army sergeant Oliver Reed offers a drink to his dance date in *Triple Echo* (1973). Played by BRIAN DEACON, "she" is actually an Army deserter, masquerading as an English farm woman's sister to avoid exposure, and to be with the woman he loves.

THUNDERBOLT AND LIGHTFOOT

In *Thunderbolt and Lightfoot* (1974), JEFF BRIDGES was a young drifter who joined seasoned thief Clint Eastwood in Montana to pull an armoury heist. Part of the intricate plan involved Bridges masquerading as a young chick to lure an over-zealous employee from his vital post.

His excellent portrayal won him a supporting Academy Award nomination.

FREEBIE AND THE BEAN

Freebie and the Bean (1974) was a trashy cops-and-robbers yarn concerning two plainclothesmen trying to get the goods on racketeer boss Jack Kruschen. Here we see Kruschen being threatened by psyched-up **CHRISTOPHER MORLEY**, in amazingly good female drag, who later meets a bloody end in a stadium ladies' room at the hands of cop Freebie (James Caan).

THE TENANT

In his murky film *The Tenant* (1976), director-actor **ROMAN POLANSKI** played a shy young man who moves into an apartment whose last tenant, a girl, left by the window. Becoming convinced that the other tenants wish him to take the dead girl's place, he assumes her identity and eventually duplicates her fate.

THE THRILLERS

EARLY SERIAL

RUTH ROLAND, the famous serial queen of the mid-teens finds herself in a triple-drag situation in one melodramatic episode.

THE OLD DARK HOUSE

Only the most astute of film buffs know that the aged man in the upstairs bedroom in James Whale's *The Old Dark House* (1932) is actually character actress ELSPETH DUDGEON, but no one knows why. She was billed as "John" Dudgeon and gives a brief but astoundingly good "drag" performance. Do you suppose Raymond Massey and Gloria Stuart know?

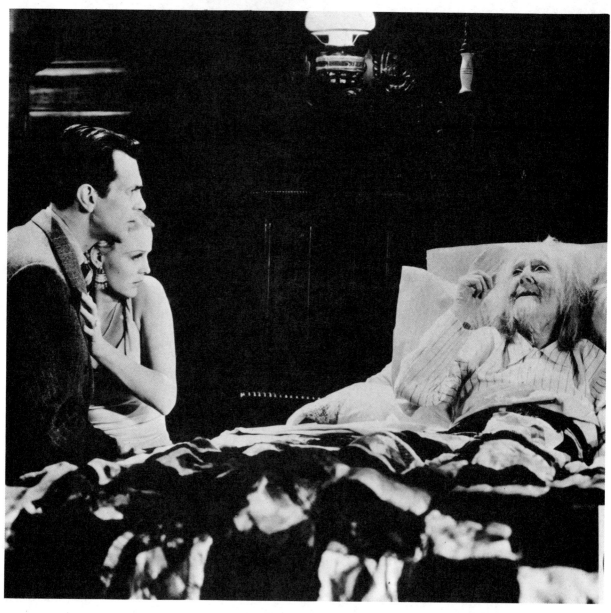

SHERLOCK HOLMES

CLIVE BROOK in *Sherlock Holmes* (1932) in one of the many disguises he adopts while portraying Conan Doyle's immortal sleuth.

THE RETURN OF SOPHIE LANG

In *The Return of Sophie Lang* (1936) GERTRUDE MICHAEL plays a reformed jewel thief trying to prove herself innocent of a robbery. Disguised as a reporter she finally gets help from friend Ray Milland.

UP THE RIVER

ARTHUR TREACHER and **PRESTON FOSTER**, while appearing in a prison show, decide how they can aid their young cellmate Tony Martin. They escape in women's apparel to "rub out" a confidence man who's putting the squeeze on Martin's mother in *Up the River* (1938). Their hitch-hiking experiences were a riot: Foster shrinks from William Irving's advances while Treacher becomes uncomfortable with Irving Bacon.

THE AMAZING MR WILLIAMS

MELVYN DOUGLAS as an officer of the homicide squad uses feminine drag to entrap a ladykiller in *The Amazing Mr Williams* (1939). Clarence Kolb, at left, is delighted by this lady's boldness as "she" puts bellhop Dave Willock in his place. Note the veil which was designed to conceal Douglas' moustache.

CLOAK AND DAGGER

LILLI PALMER, an Italian partisan in disguise as a young man, aids physics professor Gary Cooper on an OSS mission to locate an atomic scientist, in Fritz Lang's thriller *Cloak and Dagger* (1946). The pair are aided by Dan Seymour, Ramon Ros and Robert Alda.

THE MAN OF A THOUSAND FACES
&
THE UNHOLY THREE

JAMES CAGNEY began as a chorus "girl" in vaudeville but only once appeared in drag in his lengthy screen career. In the superb biographical film *The Man of a Thousand Faces* (1957) Cagney portrayed silent star Lon Chaney, a task which involved recreating many of Chaney's notable film characterisations. Here he is seen as Chaney playing "Grandmother" in *The Unholy Three*. CHANEY's original portrayal is seen underneath.

Chaney, a master of disguise throughout his career, did both a silent (1925) and talkie version (1930) of *The Unholy Three*. As an out-of-work carnival performer in the talkie version, Chaney and his friend Midget (Harry Earles) turned to a life of crime using as their cover the disguise of "Grandmother" and "Baby"

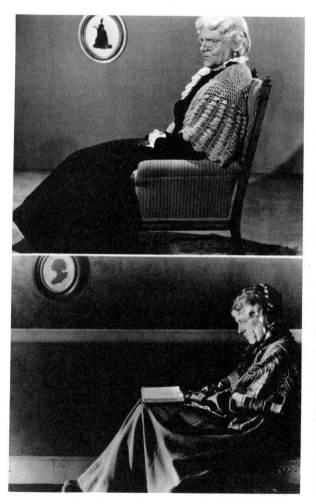

IN LIKE FLINT

Character actor LEE J. COBB gets into full drag in the tongue-in-cheek thriller *In Like Flint* (1964) playing a spy chief, with a penchant for disguises, in a yarn about a group of women trying to take control of the world.

UP TO
HIS EARS

Bored playboy JEAN-PAUL BELMONDO arranges his own death in the comic thriller *Up to His Ears* (1966) but later changes his mind. The misadventures which follow, trying to escape his assassins, include a drag striptease.

THAT MAN FROM ISTANBUL

Playboy **HORST BUCHHOLZ** is pressed into service as a spy by agent Sylva Koscina in the espionage thriller *That Man from Istanbul* (1966). Here Buchholz can be seen in one of the disguises he assumes while tracking down a missing scientist.

MODESTY BLAISE

In Joseph Losey's pop-artish and vapid *Modesty Blaise* (1966) Italian beauty ROSSELLA FALK appeared as a minister. With her here is the secret agent heroine Monica Vitti. The whole mess was based on the British comic strip.

THE KREMLIN LETTER

GEORGE SANDERS played The Warlock, an ageing San Francisco drag queen (actually a Western intelligence agent), who becomes the toast of Moscow's homosexual-literary set in an effort to find an important document of world-shaking importance, in John Huston's confusing espionage thriller *The Kremlin Letter* (1970).

THEATRE
OF
BLOOD

In *Theatre of Blood* (1973), DIANA RIGG, the daughter of a hammy Shakespearean actor played by Vincent Price, in a series of disguises aids him as he seeks revenge on eight critics who denied him a top theatrical award. In the second still Rigg and Price, as a pair of hippie hairdressers, give Coral Browne her final permanent.

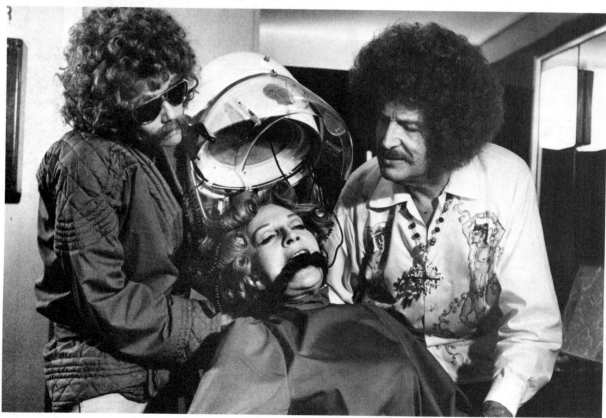

PERIOD PIECES —
Historical Drag

THE PRINCE AND THE PAUPER & OLIVER TWIST

The theatrical tradition of actresses assuming the roles of boys was most popular in movies made prior to 1922. These women played boys throughout and were *not* women characters masquerading as boys. Naturally, it was easier for audiences to accept this occurrence in an historical setting.

MARGUERITE CLARK, shown here as the pauper boy in Mark Twain's *The Prince and the Pauper* (1915) (opposite), essayed both roles.

MARIE DORO repeated her notable stage success as Charles Dickens' *Oliver Twist* (1916). (An earlier version had been filmed in England in 1912 with Ivy Millais as Oliver.) Doro can be seen here as the scruffy Oliver with Tully Marshall as Fagin and then as the smartly dressed orphan-cum-heir.

TREASURE ISLAND

In 1920 director Maurice Tourneur erred when he cast **SHIRLEY MASON** as young Jim Hawkins in Robert Louis Stevenson's adventure yarn *Treasure Island*. She gave the role a boyish charm but was not the robust lad the author had created, appearing "too feminine" to sustain the illusion.

LITTLE
LORD FAUNTLEROY

MARY PICKFORD in her elaborate production of *Little Lord Fauntleroy* (1921) appeared as Cedric, the title character, an American heir to an earldom who reconciles his grandfather to his widowed mother Dearest (also played by Miss Pickford). Seen with her here is Joseph Dowling and Claude Gillingwater as the grandfather.

WHEN KNIGHTHOOD WAS IN FLOWER, LITTLE OLD NEW YORK & BEVERLY OF GRAUSTARK

MARION DAVIES was very popular in historical romantic dramas before proving her comic skill. As Mary Tudor, younger sister of King Henry VIII in *When Knighthood was in Flower* (1921), she runs away from court, disguised as a boy, to marry commoner Forrest Stanley (at right) but first must duel a half-drunk adventurer George Nash who does not know her true identity.

In *Little Old New York* (1923) Irish lass Marion comes to America to claim a fortune left to her brother who has died en route. To do so she has to impersonate him, leaving little Helen Jerome Eddy confused.

When her royal cousin is injured in a skiing accident, Marion dons his uniform and impersonates him until he recovers. Meanwhile, Antonio Moreno (left) becomes her constant companion and guard not knowing that this young lad is really *Beverly of Graustark* (1926).

THE THIEF OF BAGDAD

When Douglas Fairbanks was casting his great Arabian Nights fantasy *The Thief of Bagdad* (1924) he could not find the right man to play the rotund Persian Prince so he chose **MATHILDE COMONT**. Billed simply as "Mat", she is shown here flanked by So-Jin as the Mongol Prince and Snitz Edwards as the thief's evil associate.

THE WARRIOR'S HUSBAND

In the historical farce *The Warrior's Husband* (1933) ERNEST TRUEX in the title role wears silks and satins, with his hair and beard in corkscrew curls, while his wife Hippolyta, Queen of the Amazons (MARJORIE RAMBEAU) and sister Antiope (ELISSA LANDI) wear the armour and protect their land from invaders. Landi and Rambeau are joined in the second scene by MAUDE EBURNE. This role-reversal comedy provided many laughs.

QUEEN CHRISTINA

GRETA GARBO as the seventeenth century Swedish heroine of *Queen Christina* (1933), whose penchant for male attire was attributed to her father's wish for an heir to his throne, romps around the countryside and meets John Gilbert, an emissary from the King of Spain.

She takes a room at a wayside inn from the innkeeper (Ferdinand Munier) and again meets the Spanish envoy who soon cautions the young man, to whom he is attracted, not to engage in a duel with a drunken lout (Edward Gargan). They become fast friends, and when the Spaniard suggests sharing the room upstairs Garbo agrees. Even the maid (Barbara Barondess) is infatuated with this handsome cavalier. It is only later that Gilbert discovers his companion is a woman and later still before he learns that she is the monarch to whom he is delivering a royal marriage proposal.

THE SCARLET PIMPERNEL

In *The Scarlet Pimpernel* (1935) LESLIE HOWARD, as the English fop Sir Percy Blakeney, dons many disguises to save aristocrats from the terror of the French Revolution. Here the resourceful Pimpernel pretends to be an old hag at a French border gate.

PEG OF OLD DRURY

In the England of 1740, headstrong Irish actress Peg Woffington, brilliantly portrayed by ANNA NEAGLE, dressed here as a young man, defends her honour in the splendid British production *Peg of Old Drury* (1935).

AS YOU LIKE IT

In Paul Czinner's production of Shakespeare's comedy *As You Like It* (1936) his wife ELISABETH BERGNER played Rosalind, the banished duke's daughter who poses as a shepherd boy in the forest of Arden to get the unwitting Orlando (Laurence Olivier) to expound on his love for her.

KNIGHT WITHOUT ARMOUR

In *Knight Without Armour* (1937) MARLENE DIETRICH, as a White Russian countess, teams up with Robert Donat, a British intelligence agent posing as a Red Russian. During the revolution Dietrich disguises herself as a cossack to avoid the firing squad.

CARDBOARD CAVALIER

British comedian SID FIELD in *Cardboard Cavalier* (1949) was a barrow-boy who gets involved in a plot against Cromwell in seventeenth century England. He is flanked by Mary Clare as Milady Doverhouse and Edmund Willard as Oliver Cromwell.

THE CRIMSON PIRATE

BURT LANCASTER (left) and his former circus partner NICK CRAVAT (right) burlesqued buccaneer pictures in *The Crimson Pirate* (1952). These formidable lads try to free a Caribbean island from royal clutches by masquerading as wenches to gain entry into the city. Once in it's a swashbuckling good time until their comrades, and the woman Lancaster loves, are free.

CASANOVA'S BIG NIGHT

In *Casanova's Big Night* (1954) BOB HOPE (as a tailor's apprentice who poses as the great lover) and JOAN FONTAINE switch roles at the ball, where the Doge's men are searching for the impostor.

FELLINI SATYRICON

Aboard ship in the world of Petronius Arbiter, Rome 50-66 AD, ALAIN CUNY (as Lica the bride) weds young Encolpio (Martin Potter) in *Fellini Satyricon* (1970). Federico Fellini's surrealistic fresco, while disturbing, is at the same time fascinating cinema.

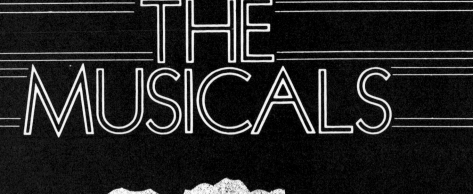

THE
MUSICALS

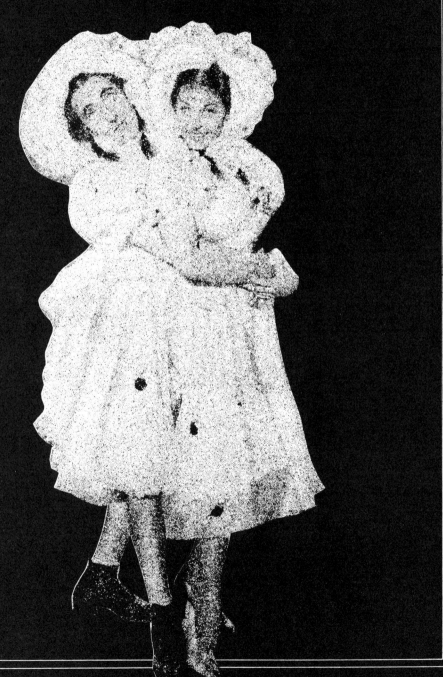

DR MABUSE DER SPIELER

Fritz Lang's 1922 German thriller *Dr Mabuse der Spieler* (*Dr Mabuse, the Gambler*) gave us a glimpse of a typical German cabaret with its deco decadence. LIL DAGOVER, in male attire and monocle, is the performer.

MOTHER KNOWS BEST

Silent star **MADGE BELLAMY** was a great mimic as witnessed by her part-talkie vaudeville film *Mother Knows Best* (1928), in which she imitated Sir Harry Lauder and Anna Held. The most adroit impersonation, however, was her stunning drag rendition of Al Jolson singing "Mammy".

LAUGHING SINNERS

As a small town cabaret entertainer in *Laughing Sinners* (1931) JOAN CRAWFORD is getting ready to go on in camp-drag as a farmer in a comedy dance routine.

BROADWAY THRU A KEYHOLE

CONSTANCE CUMMINGS (left) and **BLOSSOM SEELEY** (right) both got into chic male attire for *Broadway Thru a Keyhole* (1933), which boasted a nightclub background, racketeers, romance and some snappy Gordon and Revel songs.

ZOUZOU The glamorous JOSEPHINE BAKER as she appeared in the French film *Zouzou* (1934), a tale about a Creole laundress who romances a sailor (Jean Gabin) and finally becomes a star of the music halls.

VIKTOR UND VIKTORIA, FIRST A GIRL & VICTOR/VICTORIA

The German musical-comedy *Viktor und Viktoria* (1933) and its British re-make *First a Girl* (1935) dealt with female and male impersonation.

In the former, aspiring actress RENATE MÜLLER meets vaudeville performer HERMANN THIMIG who does an act in a local theatre in which he plays both the male character (Viktor) and the female character (Viktoria). When he becomes ill one day, Renate impersonates him and plays both parts on stage *in reverse*. Naturally, she is spotted by a big-time producer who had come to catch Hermann's act and she becomes a star with Hermann acting as her manager.

In *First a Girl* British star JESSIE MATTHEWS is the girl who substitutes for female impersonator SONNIE HALE and goes on to greater glory (opposite top).

Director Blake Edwards did the third re-make as *Victor/Victoria* (1982) with JULIE ANDREWS as a down-and-out singer who, with the help of gay entertainer ROBERT PRESTON, becomes a hit musical star playing a man playing a woman (opposite bottom). This delightful farce of mistaken identities moved the action to 1930s Paris.

MAYTIME

JEANETTE MACDONALD as a famous singer in the musical *Maytime* (1937) interprets the young page's role (always sung by a woman) from Meyerbeer's opera *Les Huguenots*.

ROSALIE

As a Balkan princess attending Vassar in *Rosalie* (1937), ELEANOR POWELL impersonates a West Point cadet to be near the young man she loves (Nelson Eddy). Here the newest cadet solos with her/his mates backing her/him up.

MOUNTAIN MUSIC

The hillbilly romp *Mountain Music* (1937)
provided ex-vaudeville performer WALLY
VERNON (seen here with Martha Raye) with
an opportunity to strut his stuff — even if it
was as Martha's sister in a musical number.

SING,
YOU SINNERS

FRED MACMURRAY in drag as Grandma
while Bing Crosby is Grandpa to young
Donald O'Connor's Small Fry — the delightful
Hoagy Carmichael-Frank Loesser number
from *Sing, You Sinners* (1938).

ARGENTINE NIGHTS, WINGED VICTORY & THE RITZ

The Andrews Sisters, Maxine, Patty and LaVerne (left), became the most popular singing trio of the forties. Their particularly campy style and unique sound came in for much imitation and parody.

It all started in one of their pictures. In *Argentine Nights* (1940) when the girls are confined to their staterooms aboard ship, the RITZ BROTHERS (Jimmy, Harry and Al) go on for them to do their rendition of "Rhumboogie" (below left).

Moss Hart's GI show *Winged Victory* (1944) gave three soldiers (JACK SLATE, RED BUTTONS and HENRY SLATE) an opportunity to entertain their buddies in a Pacific island camp show.

The girls were once again parodied in the madcap antics of *The Ritz* (1976). This time PAUL B. PRICE, JACK WESTON and F. MURRAY ABRAHAM mimed to a record in a gay bath-house contest.

POT O'GOLD   In 1941, **PAULETTE GODDARD** appeared as a male dancer in the "Broadway Caballero" number in the minor comedy *Pot O'Gold*.

BABES ON BROADWAY
&
EASTER PARADE

JUDY GARLAND made a striking boy in *Babes on Broadway* (1941) with her impersonation of the great Sarah Bernhardt in one of her best-known roles (as Napoleon's ill-fated son, the Duc de Reichstadt in *L'Aiglon*). In the same musical comedy Judy played a minstrel boy — in blackface — with Mickey Rooney.

In *Easter Parade* (1948) she and Fred Astaire appeared as a pair of bums singing and dancing to the Irving Berlin song "A Couple of Swells".

BABES ON BROADWAY, WINGED VICTORY, THE ROAD TO RIO
&
ALWAYS LEAVE THEM LAUGHING

Carmen Miranda (left), the Brazilian Bombshell, gained stature with platform shoes, enormous headdresses and a vivacious personality that provided mimics with loads of material.

MICKEY ROONEY gave the first — and one of the best — impersonations of Carmen, in all her exuberance, in "Bombshell from Brazil" from *Babes on Broadway* (1941).

In Moss Hart's *Winged Victory* (1944), SASCHA BRASTOFF repeated his inventive stage burlesque of Carmen, utilising an Army blanket, utensils, insignia, and ammunition as his costume. Carmen was thrilled and Brastoff later became her costume designer.

When his "Road" pictures took him to Rio de Janeiro it was a foregone conclusion that BOB HOPE would do a take-off of Carmen (*The Road to Rio*, 1947).

MILTON BERLE did a unique impersonation of Carmen seen here on the set of *Always Leave Them Laughing* (1949) with director Roy Del Ruth.

STAR-SPANGLED RHYTHM

In the all-star wartime musical *Star-Spangled Rhythm* (1942) glamour girls Paulette Goddard, Dorothy Lamour and Veronica Lake parodied their own screen personas with the clever number "A Sweater, A Sarong and A Peekaboo Bang" and were further satirised in a camp-drag rendition by ARTHUR TREACHER, WALTER CATLETT and STERLING HOLLOWAY.

GEORGE WHITE'S SCANDALS

Sister acts have always been audience pleasers. In *George White's Scandals* (1945) JACK HALEY appeared in full drag with Joan Davis in one of the hilarious musical numbers.

MOTHER WORE TIGHTS, THE L-SHAPED ROOM & STAR!

"Burlington Bertie", the great music hall and vaudeville favourite, written in 1914 by William Hargreaves for his wife Ella Shields, has been used often in films as a perfect song for a woman in male attire. In the forties BETTY GRABLE donned tux, top hat and monocle for her rendition of this great number in her musical *Mother Wore Tights* (1947).

In the non-musical *The L-Shaped Room* (1963) CICELY COURTNEIDGE gave a touching performance as a lesbian landlady who, to cheer up pregnant tenant Leslie Caron, dons her old music hall uniform and performs "Burlington Bertie"

Gertrude Lawrence got her first big break doing this routine in the 1918 *Charlot's Revue* as interpreted by JULIE ANDREWS in the film bio *Star!* (1968).

LAWRENCE WRIGHT'S 6D INSPIRATIONS, No 1187
THIS SONG MAY BE SUNG IN PUBLIC WITHOUT FEE OR LICENSE EXCEPT AT THEATRES AND MUSIC HALLS.
BURLINGTON BERTIE FROM BOW.
Written and Composed by
William Hargreaves
Sung by
MISS ELLA SHIELDS

ON THE TOWN

As three wild sailors on furlough in New York City in *On The Town* (1949), **FRANK SINATRA, JULES MUNSHIN** and **GENE KELLY** create havoc in a museum and flee to Coney Island with the military police in hot pursuit. The boys disguise themselves as harem girls in a sideshow and sing "Pearl of the Persian Sea" before being apprehended.

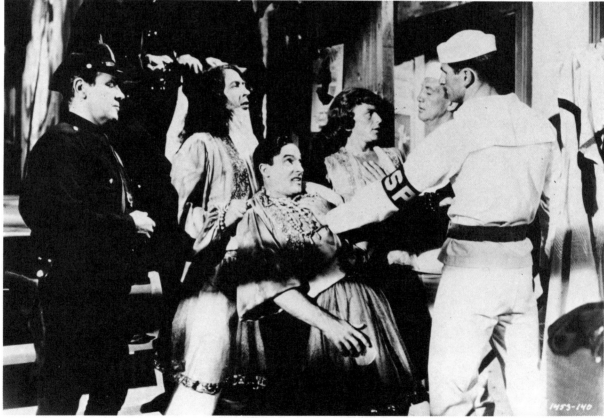

LET'S DANCE

Vivacious BETTY HUTTON (left) did a superb drag rendition of a rough cowpoke with Fred Astaire in a Western saloon setting for the "Oh Them Dudes" production number in *Let's Dance* (1950).

I'LL SEE YOU IN MY DREAMS

I'll See You in My Dreams (1951) was a romantic musical biography of lyricist Gus Kahn. DORIS DAY played his wife and can be seen here (in blackface for the Al Jolson "Toot Toot Tootsie Goodbye" number) with her real-life counterpart Mrs Gus Kahn.

WHITE CHRISTMAS

Once the leading ladies of *White Christmas* (1954) finish the sassy song "Sisters", BING CROSBY and DANNY KAYE come out in camp-drag and give it a try!

SAYONARA

The romantic drama *Sayonara* (1957) presented contrasts in Japanese theatrical history. **RICARDO MONTALBAN**, as a star of the all-male Kabuki theatre, prepares himself for a scene as a delicate Geisha girl. **MIIKO TAKA**, on the other hand, as a member of the Matsubayashi Girl Revue, does a modern turn as a man in top hat, white tie and tails.

THE PAJAMA GAME

In the film version of the hit Broadway musical *The Pajama Game* (1957), CAROL HANEY becomes part of a male trio for the "Steam Heat" number.

SOUTH PACIFIC

In the Rodgers and Hammerstein musical *South Pacific* (1958), audiences were treated to a double drag as MITZI GAYNOR, as the sailor, sings to RAY WALSTON, as the native girl, in the "Honey Bun" number.

DER ROSENKAVALIER

The art of impersonation is not new to the world of opera. In Paul Czinner's filmed version of Richard Strauss' opera *Der Rosenkavalier* (1962), SENA JURINAC is the young man Octavian (traditionally sung by a woman) who becomes romantically involved with Sophie (sung by Anneliese Rothenberger).

THE
CHORUS LINES

KIKI **MARY PICKFORD** as the klutzy chorine in *Kiki* (1931) gets out of place from the other "gentlemen" of the chorus and lands directly in front of the show's star Margaret Livingston.

BEST OF ENEMIES

Charles "Buddy" Rogers as a composer in *Best of Enemies* (1933) directs his score as the chorus "girls" of the show await their cue in the dress rehearsal.

SWEET MUSIC

These college boys are doing the best they can as chorus "girls" in the big campus show for *Sweet Music* (1935), but Rudy Vallee conducting his orchestra in the background doesn't seem to mind.

LE GRANDE ILLUSION

Jean Gabin interrupts the prisoner-of-war drag chorus entertainment with the exciting news that the French have recaptured from the Germans one of their towns, in Jean Renoir's superb anti-war film *Le Grande Illusion* (1937).

THIS IS
THE ARMY

ALAN HALE cavorts with an all-soldier group in the "Ladies of the Chorus" production number from Irving Berlin's *This is the Army* (1943).

IRISH EYES
ARE SMILING

For the final production number in *Irish Eyes are Smiling* (1944) lovely JUNE HAVER became the leading man while the boys became the chorus "girls".

STAR! JULIE ANDREWS, and two members of the "soldier" chorus, in one of the World War I routines from the laboured Gertrude Lawrence biopic *Star!* (1968).

PAPER LION

These strapping football players (all members of the famed Detroit Lions team) made up the chorus line for a bit of fun in *Paper Lion* (1968), based on George Plimpton's book.

THE WESTERNS

NUGGET NELL

In her delightful burlesque of the standard western hero, silent star **DOROTHY GISH** had a comic field day as *Nugget Nell* (1919). Here co-star Raymond Cannon begs Nell to save the day in a funny role-reversal situation.

LADY ROBINHOOD

In *Lady Robinhood* (1925), EVELYN BRENT, the lovely ward of a Spanish governor, disguises herself as the masked bandit, La Ortiga, battling injustice, helping the poor and plotting a revolution to overthrow the corrupt officials.

SEÑORITA

BEBE DANIELS, after being brought up in the US, returns to her grandfather's South American hacienda to aid the old man in his fight against outlaws, in *Señorita* (1927). She disguises herself as a young Zorro-type and, with some fancy sword play, wins the fight.

CAUGHT
&
CALAMITY JANE

Two interpretations of the same real-life character, Calamity Jane, are seen here. LOUISE DRESSER portrayed her as a mannish woman who leads a man's existence in *Caught* (1931), while DORIS DAY made her a tomboy who would change her "ways" for the right man in the musical comedy *Calamity Jane* (1953).

WEST OF THE PECOS

Zane Grey's *West of the Pecos* gave the leading lady the chance to shear her hair and pretend she was a boy because "no woman was safe on the streets of San Antonio".

MARTHA SLEEPER (seen here with Richard Dix) was the disguised boy in the 1934 version, while BARBARA HALE essayed the role in the 1945 re-make (here with Thurston Hall and Mara Corday).

ZORRO'S BLACK WHIP

After her brother is killed in the twelve-chapter serial *Zorro's Black Whip* (1944), LINDA STERLING assumes his identity as "The Whip" and, with the help of good guy George Lewis, cleans up the crime-ridden range.

SAN ANTONIO

Due to the wartime shortage of males, stunt lady **VIRGINIA ENGELS** played two roles in the western *San Antonio* (1945). She was a saloon hostess and also an old man who rubberishly fell down a flight of stairs during one of the film's fight scenes.

WEST
OF SONORA

SMILEY BURNETTE, Gene Autry's delightful sidekick in scores of westerns, had a ball going on as the leading lady in the local saloon's show in *West of Sonora* (1947).

MONTANA BELLE

Not all women in the old west wore bonnets and gingham dresses. JANE RUSSELL, as the outlaw Belle Starr, joined the Dalton brothers (Forrest Tucker and Scott Brady) holding up banks in *Montana Belle* (1952).

THE SHAKIEST GUN IN THE WEST

In *The Shakiest Gun in the West* (1968) DON KNOTTS is a timid Philadelphia dentist out west. After a series of a misadventures, which includes a disguise as an Indian squaw (here with Barbara Rhoades), he ultimately becomes the hero.

THE MISSOURI BREAKS

Lawman **MARLON BRANDO**, in one of his wild attempts to get outlaw Jack Nicholson, dons a woman's disguise complete with sun bonnet, in the western drama *The Missouri Breaks* (1976).

THE
CHILDREN

A BOY OF FLANDERS

JACKIE COOGAN, the biggest child star in the twenties, played a poor unwanted lad in *A Boy of Flanders* (1924). Unable to see his girl friend because of her harsh father, Jackie dresses up as a girl to attend her party but is discovered when he gets sick after eating too many chocolate cakes.

TWO GIRLS WANTED

JANET GAYNOR, as a young girl disguised as a boy to get employment in the big city, is challenged by the neighbourhood's gang in *Two Girls Wanted* (1927), before being rescued by a businessman.

PARAMOUNT ON PARADE

One of the hits of the all-star revue *Paramount on Parade* (1930) was eight-year-old **MITZI GREEN** who delightfully imitated Maurice Chevalier (who was also in the picture) in formal male attire.

WILD BOYS
OF THE ROAD

Rather than remain burdens to their depression-ridden families, boys and girls took to the road in William A. Wellman's startling *Wild Boys of the Road* (1933). Here DOROTHY COONAN, after killing a man in self defence, joins her friends Edwin Phillips (left) and Frankie Darro, disguised as a boy to avoid arrest.

CURLY TOP As the biggest child star of the thirties, **SHIRLEY TEMPLE** could do no wrong. In *Curly Top* (1935) she was an adopted orphan enjoying the pleasures of the mansion to which she has come to live. Her impersonation of an old man added laurels to her comic and musical reputation.

OUR GANG

The delightful Our Gang comedies (221 of them) usually reflected the joys, sorrows and adventures of childhood in the twenty-two years they were produced.

In an early silent JOE COBB dresses up (and what kid hasn't?) along with Farina, Johnny Downs and MICKEY DANIELS (also in drag).

Putting on a play is another pastime of children as the second scene demonstrates — with at least one of the gang playing an old lady.

NANCY DREW AND THE HIDDEN STAIRCASE

In *Nancy Drew and the Hidden Staircase* (1939) FRANKIE THOMAS, as Bonita Granville's ever-present companion, does everything he can to assist the girl-detective, even if it means masquerading in female garb to aid spinsters being victimised by crooks. Here the resourceful pair are being helped by John Litel and Frank Orth.

MEET ME IN ST LOUIS

With other kids on the block, DARRYL HICKMAN (who couldn't decide on being a man or a woman) and MARGARET O'BRIEN don their disguises for a Hallowe'en night of trick-or-treating in *Meet Me in St Louis* (1944).

NATIONAL VELVET

As Velvet Brown in *National Velvet* (1944)
ELIZABETH TAYLOR disguised herself as a
jockey, with help from Mickey Rooney, so she
could ride her horse to victory in the Grand
National. Unfortunately she was disqualified
once it was learned that she was not a "he".

THE CHRISTINE JORGENSEN STORY

EDDIE FRANK, like so many young children, enjoys the private world of masquerade, especially when parents are absent. Here his mother (Ellen Clark) explains to George that little boys do not wear dresses and use lipstick in *The Christine Jorgensen Story* (1970).

As a grownup JOHN HANSEN as George feels "trapped in the wrong body" and undergoes a transsexual operation and subsequent treatment in Denmark. We see him here before and after. In the final moments of this dignified low-key filming of Miss Jorgensen's book, a kindly Danish aunt (Joan Tompkins) helps Christine with her new wardrobe following surgery.

THE QUEEN

The Queen (1968) was a remarkable documentary giving an insight into one aspect of America's male homosexual sub-culture — The Miss All-America Camp Beauty Pageant held at New York's Town Hall in 1967. Transvestites and female impersonators from all over the country competed.

JACK DOROSHOW, one of the leading characters (Flawless Sabrina), is shown in his dressing room and, later, performing on stage.

MYRA BRECKENRIDGE

In the tasteless *Myra Breckenridge* (1970), RAQUEL WELCH played a naval officer who has a sex-change operation and is transformed into the title character.

FORTUNE AND MEN'S EYES

Going on the theory that prisons breed criminals and deviates, *Fortune and Men's Eyes* (1971) had a diverse group crammed into a single cell. The insecure newcomer who must fight for survival; the weak member who needs protection; the bully and, of course, the carefree flamboyant type.

MICHAEL GREER played Queenie, an uninhibited homosexual, who has not only adapted to prison life but capitalised on it. Here Greer entertains fellow prisoners with a drag show in one of the film's lighter moments.

I WANT
WHAT I WANT

I Want What I Want (1972) presented ANNE HEYWOOD as Roy, a bright and decent lad, whose agonised loneliness as a boy forces him to withdraw from his widowed father's world and create his own, dressed as a woman. All is fine with "Wendy", his new identity, until a sexual attack convinces him that he must undergo a transsexual operation. Heywood's restrained approach, along with a good script and tight direction, made this a film milestone, despite its pat ending.

WOMEN IN REVOLT

CANDY DARLING, a society deb from Long Island, is shown here with her agent Michael Sklar who helps her become a movie star in Andy Warhol's mad comment on women's lib, *Women in Revolt* (1972). Since the three heroines of this tawdry piece were female impersonators, the "comment" could be interpreted as a "put-down".

PINK FLAMINGOS

Pink Flamingos: A Trip Through Decadence (1973) found its inspiration in the underground films of the 1950s and 1960s. Its star (shown here) was female impersonator DIVINE as a predatory female.

THE ROCKY HORROR PICTURE SHOW

The Rocky Horror Picture Show (1975) was a mad take-off on horror films, in a rock musical setting.

TIM CURRY as the transvestite Frank-N-Furter, gave an astonishingly fine performance. We see him in pensive mood, then singing "The Charles Atlas Song" to his new "creation" Rocky (Peter Hinwood) while Little Nell attends to her duties.

Later Frank-N-Furter and members of his staff do a production number in his ballroom. With mad scenes like these is it any wonder that this has become a cult film since its first release?

OUTRAGEOUS

In the special Canadian film *Outrageous* (1977) CRAIG RUSSELL is a gay hairdresser from Toronto with a gift for mimicry which eventually brings him to New York City as a female impersonator. He can be seen here as "Mae West" with David McIlwraith.

LA CAGE AUX FOLLES

An outlandish drag reversal occurs in the uproarious French-Italian production *La Cage aux Folles* (*Birds of a Feather*) (1979). **MICHEL SERRAULT**, as a drag queen star, and long time lover of nightclub owner Ugo Tognazzi, greets Michel Galabru, the father of the girl who wishes to marry Tognazzi's twenty-year-old son. Here Serrault is pretending to be the boy's *mother*! Later, as this funny boulevard farce unfolds, **GALABRU**, the prominent Chairman of a national decency league, is given a new identity by Serrault in order to evade hostile reporters thirsting for scandal.

In the delightful sequel *La Cage aux Folles II*, Ugo Tognazzi, proprietor of the transvestite cabaret, explains to Michel Serrault that a younger performer has been hired to impersonate Marlene Dietrich in the show.

To prove that he can still be alluring in female attire Serrault promenades in public the next day. Unwittingly, he becomes involved with a young spy, Gianrico Tondinelli, who, in fleeing a rival gang, takes Serrault to a hotel unaware that he is really a man in drag!

TELEVISION DRAG

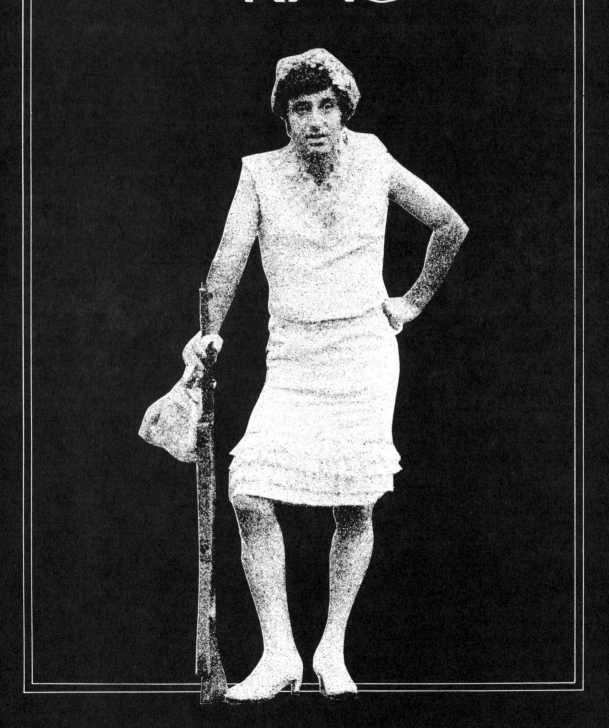

BORIS KARLOFF

BORIS KARLOFF disguised as Mother Muffin, a leader of a notorious spy ring, in "The Mother Muffin Affair" episode of the short-lived TV series *The Girl from UNCLE* (1966).

WALTER BRENNAN

Character actor WALTER BRENNAN in "The Day They Hanged Kid Curry" appeared as an ex-con artist who disguises himself as the grandmother of a jailbird in order to sneak a gun into him. He is seen here with Ben Murphy, left, and Pete Duel in this 1971 episode of the series *Alias Smith and Jones*.

RICH LITTLE

When Tony Curtis was guest host on ABC's *The Kopykats* in 1972, impressionist RICH LITTLE joined him in a scene from Curtis' movie *Some Like It Hot*.

MILTON BERLE

MILTON BERLE, a "drag" expert in his early television shows, can be seen here as a sassy Spanish señorita with Bob Hope in *Murder at NBC* — a Bob Hope Comedy Special.

FLIP WILSON
&
SAMMY DAVIS, JR

Comedian **FLIP WILSON**'s masterful drag character "Geraldine Jones" became a delightful mainstay of his television show. Geraldine can be seen here in a 1975 show with guest Sammy Davis, Jr.

SAMMY DAVIS, JR has previously appeared in drag (with *Laugh-In*'s **ARTE JOHNSON**) in the 1973 revue *The NBC Follies*.

LORI SHANNON

It was only a matter of time before bigot Archie Bunker, brilliantly portrayed by Carroll O'Connor in the TV series *All in the Family*, would meet a female impersonator. After saving **LORI SHANNON**'s life, Archie discovers to his dismay that she's no lady in this 1975 episode.

HARVEY KORMAN

HARVEY KORMAN was always adding to the mirth of the outstanding variety programme *The Carol Burnett Show* with drag impersonations. Here Korman (centre) is joined by Vicki Lawrence and Carol Burnett to make a jazzy trio.

LES BALLETS TROCKADERO DE MONTE CARLO

SHIRLEY MACLAINE (centre) is surrounded by members of the drag group, Les Ballets Trockadero de Monte Carlo, in a number from her 1977 TV special, *Where Do We Go from Here?*

STANLEY BAXTER

Scottish comedian **STANLEY BAXTER** is seen here as a maid on Bing Crosby's final television show, which was taped in England just prior to the latter's death in 1977.

HENRY WINKLER

HENRY WINKLER, as Fonzie, becomes his own mother when he attends his funeral on an episode of the popular show *Happy Days*. His close friends Laverne and Shirley (Penny Marshall and Cindy Williams) can hardly contain their grief as they stare at all that's supposed to be left of him — a motorcycle boot and crowbar. Tom Bosley looks on.

JAMIE FARR In the popular TV series M*A*S*H (Mobile Army Surgical Hospital), JAMIE FARR, a misfit Army corporal in Korea, continually dresses up in drag in a mad attempt to get a psycho discharge. But everyone is so caught up in the insanity of war that no one takes him seriously.

HOLLYWOOD AT PLAY

FLORADORA GIRLS

ED WYNN, EDDIE CANTOR, BORIS KARLOFF, VINCENT PRICE and **CLIFTON WEBB** make an unlikely quintet of Floradora Girls for a charity benefit at Hollywood's famed Masquer's Club in the late 1940s. Here the "girls" take a break before strutting their stuff!

MARIE WILSON

During a break in the filming of *Boy Meets Girl* (1938), MARIE WILSON plays Charlie McCarthy to James Cagney's Edgar Bergen in a skit for a studio show.

BETTE DAVIS   During World War II, at the Hollywood
Canteen (which she co-founded), BETTE
DAVIS helps entertain the GIs with an
impersonation of Groucho Marx.

ELSA MAXWELL

In its golden age Hollywood notables threw grand parties. At one of Jock Whitney's costume affairs famed hostess **ELSA MAXWELL** (in drag as a man) greeted Carole Lombard who arrived on a stretcher. Other guests included Delmer Daves, Kay Francis, Virginia Bruce and Countess Dorothy de Frasso as a nun.

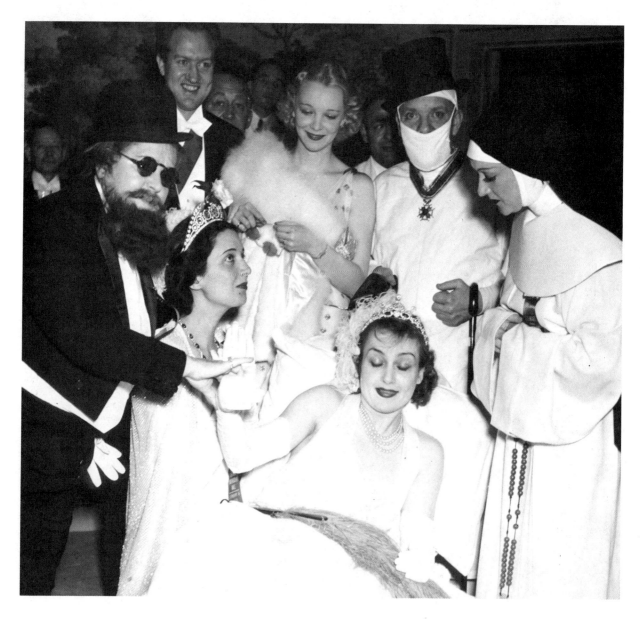

INDEX OF PERFORMERS IN DRAG